Meditations on God and the Soul

Edward Conklin Ph.D.

Copyright 2015 by Edward Conklin. All Rights Reserved.

This book or any portion thereof may not be reproduced or used in any manner including any electronic or mechanical information storage and retrieval systems, without the express permission of the publisher. Scanning, uploading, photocopying, and facilitating the electronic distribution of this book without permission of the publisher is prohibited.

ISBN 978-0-9906457-6-4

Edward Conklin

Dedication

I dedicate this work to the young, who not told, usually have to find out the hard way.

Edward Conklin

Acknowledgments

I gratefully acknowledge and thank family, friends, and teachers for their love and encouragement. I am indebted to many who have come before and without whose tireless efforts, findings, and recorded words, this work would not have been written. I acknowledge and thank Ms. Natalie Harley for her editorial assistance and patience.

Edward Conklin

Published works by Edward Conklin Ph.D.

Psychology of God and the Soul. (2016). Amazon Kindle and CreateSpace.

Meditations on God and the Soul. (2015). Amazon Kindle and CreateSpace.

A Brief Guide to God and the Soul. (2015). Amazon Kindle and CreateSpace.

In the Beginning: A New Theory of the First Religion. (2014). Amazon Kindle and CreateSpace.

Cosmos, God, and Soul. (2014). Amazon Kindle and CreateSpace.

From Tool-maker to God Maker. (2014). Amazon Kindle and CreateSpace.

Waves Rough and Smooth & the Deep Blue Sea. (2014). Amazon Kindle and CreateSpace.

Getting Back Into the Garden of Eden. (1998). University Press of America.

Edward Conklin

Introduction

Writing is either an individual obsession, possession by a muse, or a combination of both. In either scenario, the practice of meditation as a fixing of attention on a topic for the purpose of better comprehension of it, is a helpful discipline to any aspiring individual desirous of communicating through the written word.

The English word meditation is derived from the Latin word meditatio, meaning, to think, ponder, reflect in thought, muse, and to ruminate. Yet the word meditation has a more specific meaning, and that is to focus attention for the purpose of reducing the flowing stream of conscious ideational images of remembering, imagining, and reasoning. The desired result is to arrive at genuine perception and insight.

Clear comprehension can be cultivated through meditation, yet many lack interest and knowledge of the practice. Instead, the mass majority are distracted by the daily task of survival, and by the panoramic show that life presents on a daily basis. There are many shows the individual can attend in life, such as antique, art, fashion, gun, television, and movie shows. Substitutes for meditation and peace of mind, are shopping, eating, possessing, and arguing. There are myriad activities and entertainments but few individuals have the time or the ability to focus attention and to meditate.

A child moves toys around a bedroom and a house. During a lifetime an adult acquires and moves possessions around to a number of locales. A curious and intelligent person has little interest in or time for toys or many possessions. If mature, he may reach a time and stage of life where he loses interest in having and moving around possessions, and perhaps then may begin to ponder what unknown force moves the known universe and himself into, through and out of existence. Sensing a limit to his lifetime, he may then devote some time to explore and to better comprehend the mythos of a human-like god and a human soul. What follows are meditations on these two metaphysical topics.

Knowing God

The Hindu saint, Ramakrishna (1836-1886) made the statement, "He is born in vain who, having attained the human birth, so difficult to get, does not attempt to realize God in this very life." These are inspiring words uttered by the saint Ramakrishna, yet challenging and difficult for an individual to achieve. Most humans have little time to investigate, and even less time to realize what a god is. Instead, the average person settles for and relies on faith, belief, and tradition to provide meager evidence for the existence of a human-like god.

The meditations that follow serve to elucidate the long held conception of a human-like god. Rather than indulge in idle and unrewarding speculation and abstract ideas about a human-like god as an objective reality, the following meditative discussions are based on investigative perceptions and how a human-like god is a dynamic of human subjective imagining that begins in childhood and extends through adulthood.

Imaginary Companion

Studies show that close to seventy percent of children have had an imaginary friend or companion that they interacted with during play. A child's imaginary companion can be a child, adult, animal, monster, ghost, or a relative. A child may spontaneously speak of an imaginary companion usually in the range of from two through nine years of age. This innate developmental cognitive process fades during the maturation process of adjusting to a cause and effect objective reality. More females have imaginary companions than do male children.

A child spontaneously imagines a companion as a way of playing, having fun, self-expression, exploring, learning, and practicing relationship interaction. An imaginary companion is not the result of isolation, a failure to socialize, or a psychological disorder. Having an imaginary companion or friend is a way of practicing communication when a child's friends or peers are not readily available.

When there is a delay or lack of interaction with others, the child may then spontaneously make up an imaginary companion. A child's imaginary companion is usually invisible, though may also include projecting a personality onto toys. An imaginary companion is often helpful and even protective. Interaction with an imaginary companion provides comfort and relief from difficulties of adjustment, and companionship when afraid or alone. An imaginary companion may approve or disapprove of the child's behaviors, and thus function as a conscience, a guide of right or wrong. These features and benefits of a child's imaginary companion, strongly match the role of a human-like god for adults.

The spontaneous strength of the childhood tendency to have an imaginary companion, may endure and continue to exert a subconscious predisposition later in adult life. Previously having had an imaginary companion, may predispose and so cause some individuals to be susceptible and receptive to, and to more easily accept the theistic view of a friendly companion, a human-like god. The childhood phenomenon of an imaginary companion suggests evidence of incipient theism, and the later adult acceptance of a human-like god. The evidence at least suggests that theistic religion with its imagined human-like god, is a continuation of this innate childhood developmental process.

Just as many children have an imaginary companion they interact with, so do adults have an imaginary god companion who is friendly to them. Research shows that upwards of two-thirds of children have had an imaginary companion. There may well be a correlation of this finding with other findings that variously show over two-thirds of the adult population accept the view of a human-like god. Some forty percent or more of the population in the United States gather regularly in a public religious building to meet and to share the imaginary companion of a numerical first father god. Research also finds more females have an imaginary companion; speculatively, there may be a correlation with studies that show in general, a higher number of women attend religious services than do men.

What is not real and is only imaginary can serve a real and useful purpose. An imaginary Santa Claus is useful through the year as a creative way to encourage unruly children to be good, receiving either a reward or punishment on the day of Christmas. The imaginary Santa also arrives on the birthday of the supposed son of a human-like god. An imaginary Easter Bunny who brings eggs, through colorful artistic images usefully communicates a real renewing of life in the spring time of the year. For the real disfiguring loss of a tooth, an imaginary fairy compensates a child with a reward of real money left under a pillow.

Human adult life is permeated with imagining. Visual art is the making of images that are imaginary copies of the environment and life but are not real. The drama of theater plays and movies are based on imaginary characters, as are fiction books. The many adventure and super heroes are imaginary. The innate development of an imaginary companion in childhood, and the historical predisposition to imagine a human-like first father god, has coevolved with and been succeeded by this pandemic plethora of artistic imagination.

Imagining is not completely relinquished as children mature and reach adulthood. Most of adult waking life consists of imagined fictions of situations and relationships that are often found too late to be disappointingly painful. Life turns out to not be the future so optimistically imagined.

The onset of the innate ability for creative imagination is comforting to a child. Yet both maturation and encountering the seriousness of life and death experience, eventually corrects the creative childhood expression of an imaginary companion. However, the tendency for having an imaginary companion is not completely forgotten. The trait is continued in the immature adult conception of the greater origin of the environment and life to be an imaginary companion of a human-like god. The childhood imago of an imaginary friend, in adulthood is transformed into an imago dei, the image of a human-like god of theism.

A human-like god is not an objective truth, rather is a pragmatic and useful subjective truth. A human-like god furnishes an explanation for the origin of existence that any average person can comprehend. A human-like first father is a conceived symbolic shortcut, fashioned by combining the numeral one with human genealogical origin. An imagined protective parent figure is a useful social rallying point for an individual and a culture.

Prayers to an imaginary god is a way of doing something to cause or effect a harmony during the disorder of an accident, illness, mistake, or relationship. An appeal is made to impose, regulate, or restore the prior order, or to remove disorder. The conscientious effort to please the imaginary companion of a human-like god, is an attempt to direct cause and effect for the better and to avoid the worst of life's offerings. To "goddam" something, is an appeal to a human-like god for assistance to stop something from happening, to dam up the situation or event.

Some studies show a negative correlation, that the more education a person has, the less religious. The educated have a glimmer of objective knowledge that through history, the brain/mind has shaped much of human reality through invention and art, including the creative imagining of various cultures that produce their own human-like gods.

An imaginary companion in childhood is subconsciously continued into adulthood to be consciously and imaginatively expressed to be a human-like god. The founders of religions who have made use of the concept of a human-like god and first father, were undoubtedly immature. The theistic religions continue to appeal to the immature of today, through lo these many years. The misleading metaphor and mistaken idea of a human-like first father god, continues to be appealing, though estimates vary, for at least fifty percent of the earth's population, and nine out of ten persons in the United States.

As with a child, the imaginary companion of a human-like god contributes to adult development. If humans imagine and accept there is a higher ego of a human-like god, then humans are inspired to elevate themselves.

A child benefits from interaction with an imaginary companion, and so does an adult benefit from interaction with the imaginary companion of a human-like god. Likewise, as do some children, theists may seek to convince others their imaginary companion is real. Yet in reality, faith (Latin fidere, trust) or trust pertains only to a subjective and imaginary human-like god. An imaginary companion of a child and the adult imaginary companion of a human-like god is a subjectively real idea in the conscious brain/mind but not objectively real outside of the brain.

An imaginary god is useful as it reduces fear. However, the usefulness of all things eventually wears out, ages, and comes to an end. The philosopher Friedrich Nietzsche (1844-1900) wrote "Gott ist tot," meaning "God is dead." Nietzsche suggests that someday in the future, humans will bring to an end, will kill off, the role model of a human-like god. This will undoubtedly happen through developmental maturation of the species, and consequent ceasing to imagine it. No longer will human attention jump to an imaginary mental model of a human-like god for refuge and protection during times of trouble.

In religions that promote a human-like god, children are trained to switch attention to an imaginary like god when interaction or help from fellow humans is lacking, or when life is threatened or overwhelmed. Children are taught to switch attention to the numerical first father origin of humans. It is supposed that if a god created humans, then surely he must continue to care for them and want to help them, especially if a person directs attention and requests the god to do so. During difficult and troubling times, both children and adults switch attention to an imaginary companion.

The childhood phenomenon of an imaginary companion, and an adulthood imaginary human-like god, are unarguably evidence of a related and prevalent continuing process of creative imagination. The spontaneous developmental stage of an imaginary companion during childhood is later in adulthood enhanced artistically with words.

The words communicated by a child to an imaginary companion is often told in short story form to curious adult listeners, and in adulthood, becomes mental or spoken aloud words of prayer to an imaginary god, supplemented by imaginative artistic scriptural stories.

God as Art

A human-like god is an artistic expression of creative imagination and talent. Religion is not a science nor is it mathematics, therefore it must logically be classified and included among the visual and verbal arts. A human-like god is an artistically imagined and word erected mentally sculptured object.

For many, individual life is made more tolerable by accepting the theological artistic word portrait of a human-like god. The Middle Eastern derived western god of theistic religion must be studied for what it really is, a creative and imaginative subjective artistic expression.

Most religious writings are vague and contradictory. This is so as they are artistic works painted with concepts and words that are poorly chinked together. The often disparate conceived ideas and words of religious story that purport to portray the acts of a human-like god, are on close examination, like the many detectable brush strokes on a canvas painting, or the chisel and sanded marks that can be observed in the work of a stone sculpture. Like so many brush strokes and metal chisel marks, over time religious authors have crafted theistic religious writings into an artistic word portrait of a human-like god.

During the previous millennia, the southwest American Indian tribes, such as the Hopi, Zuni, Pueblo and Navajo, developed the artistic practice of making colorful sand paintings. The paintings are fashioned using varying colors of sand, including white, yellow, red, blue, brown, pink, and the use of roots and tree barks. The paintings are made for the purpose of healing an ill person who is instructed to sit in the center of the work. The image content of the dry sand paintings are the yeibicheii, meaning holy people.

Prior to and during the ritual, the medicine man will chant, asking the supernatural beings to enter the likeness in the painting, and in this way their energy presence will heal the ill person. This is precisely the function of an artistic word portrait of a biblical human-like god. A biblical human-like first father god, is a conceived mental work of art to escape from the illnesses and troubles of life. The god is appealed to through prayer to heal the illness and sufferings of living, and to bring about health and wellbeing.

Until recently, most humans could only speak of their origin to be a human-like god. Much more so in the past, yet even into the twenty-first century, to dare question the notion of whether a human-like god exists, is deemed blasphemous. The person is thought by others to be seriously doomed and to be on his own in life and after death. This instilled existential fear usually results in a termination of any probing questions and serious critical investigation of the origin of existence.

A god is a conceived focal symbol for humans to think of their origin in a strictly human way. The idea of a human-like god is a psychologically conceived rallying point that serves to identify the origin of existence. Focusing on a god, humans can gather together to speak of a shared common origin. In reality, this is a psychological way of huddling with each other out of fear and helplessness. Sharing the view of a human-like god is a way of finding support, strength, and safety through the unsafe experiences of life and the anticipation of death, by orienting to a numerical first father.

Humans seek to rise above the struggles and sufferings of life, toward what isn't life, beyond struggle and suffering, and toward what does not suffer yet is human-like. Theistic religion offers to explain what is before and after life, and how to get through it. Theism also offers an explanation for existence that consists of mere brief details of an unobserved miraculous making of the environment and life presented in written words and story.

In contrast, modern science offers comprehensive written details based on observation, research, and testing of the existing geological record and fossils of life.

A human-like god who has orchestrated a miraculous beginning is subjectively conceived in human thought and then believed to be real and objective. A human-like god has a dual role; the god is accepted to be the cause of life and also functions as an ethics officer over humans. For some, merely thinking of a human-like god, supports and contributes to the fortitude and survival of an individual and enables them to continue living through a host of troubles.

Similar to talking about the arrival of Santa Claus or the Easter Bunny, the mention of a human-like god sets up an expectation of imagined special attention and reward that will hopefully soon arrive. In reality, these extraordinary personalities come only from human artistic imagination of the brain. Santa Claus and the Easter Bunny are provided by adults mainly for kids, while a human-like god is provided by theologians and adherent theists mainly for under educated and immature adults.

The Syrian philosopher-poet Al Ma'arri (973-1058 CE) poses a question about theistic religion, and then gives his answer:

"What is religion?
It is like a maiden kept close so no eye may examine her;
Just how much wealth and gifts she receives from those who woo her, is not known."

Al Ma'arri's words suggest that those who purvey theistic religion prefer to keep its dogmatic tenets subjectively close, and are not open to close examination and discussion of them, especially its teaching of a human-like god. He also suggests that organized religion amasses much unaccountable wealth from those attracted to it through donations, tithing, wills and estates.

Those who woo the human-like god of theistic religions, seek assurance and safety in life and death.

Religion offers showy rituals that attract many, and performing shared religious rituals comfort those who participate with at least the certain knowledge of what will happen next during the service. During ritual, comfort is also derived by a group mass appeal to what is experientially unknown, is only conceived and generally agreed upon, and is superficially known to be a first human-like god.

For theists, the protection of an imagined human-like god is better than relying on the real undependable protection of fellow humans, or even worse, the reality of no protection. Theistic religion is somewhat similar to a criminal protection racket. As long as the individual pays or donates, he is assured of acceptance and protection by he who acts on behalf of a human-like god father. This eerie similarity begs a question, could the structure of the Roman Catholic Church have at least in part inspired the business model of the organization known as the Mafia?

Humans mentally stick a human-like god everywhere, at the beginning of the environment and life, over the events in a person's existence, and at the end of life. This theophanous activity by humans begs a question, where will theists stick a human-like god next? Sticking the god everywhere, or omnipresence, there is no other possible place to stick it.

Invisibly larger than all of visible reality, humans cannot even think of a spot where the human-like god is not. By sticking the presence of a human-like god everywhere, humans guarantee themselves continued safety during life and death, protected by a grand and great forefather. Appearing only in the brain, humans have fathered, mothered, given birth to and nurtured the theophany and purely imaginary companion of a first father god. This is why the Middle East derived and western accepted human-like god is not visible; it resides unseen only in the human brain as an imaginary companion.

A realistic prayer for personal forgiveness may be expressed in the following words.

"O' numinous cosmos, origin of my body and brain, I ask truth to forgive me for my projection of an imaginary companion of a human-like god, for since childhood I have been in error. Having matured, I now realize that my real subconscious triune soul of the body and its wicked ways of hunger for food, sex and reproduction, and aggression, has separated me from the higher potential of my own conscious cerebral cortex. Thank you."

A theophany, the appearance of a human-like god to humans, first occurred long ago only in the human brain as an imaginary companion. There was further artistic imaginative elaboration to conceive a first unearthly father of the genealogical line of earthly fathers. The god has also made a debut in human thought as the unseen cause of the behaviors of the environment and weather. The sensed presence, vision, or dream of a deceased relative or friend has also been widely cited as evidence of rejoining with a god in a supernatural afterlife dimension. A human-like god and an afterlife are not synonymous, they are antonyms. A human-like god is imaginary and false, and an afterlife dimension is real and true.

In reality, a human-like god will never assist humans in the mysterious journey of life and death. Only the subjective idea of an imaginary companion can assist humans in tolerating life and what unknown awaits after death. Lacking personal experience, each individual develops an acceptance about what they think will happen after physical death. Some favor the view that after the body dies oblivion occurs. The other main view, is that what has animated the body in life departs and enters into the dimension of an afterlife. Either way, both possible experiences offer relief and rest from the toil and turmoil of the physical body and sufferings of life.

The conscious cerebral cortex has fabricated and placed an imaginary companion, a human-like ruling god over the human population to protect it from the environment, and from their own soul. The cerebral cortex has also with excessive pride placed a crown on its place as the uppermost important part of the human body.

In reality, the conscious cerebral cortex and central nervous system of voluntary movement, has been evolved by the subconscious autonomic nervous system of involuntary function of the cerebellum and midbrain neurons, and cells of the body.

The importance of the human soul has been long obscured by many perplexed humans who have commonly assented to accept the imaginary companion of a human-like god. Rather than a self-journey of learning and individual effort of comprehension, the imaginary companion of a human-like god has been accepted as most important and as an easy way to avoid self and soul responsibility. A human-like god is promoted as having control of the universe and can save the individual if he or she accepts the proposition, has faith, and financially supports the religious group. Yet in reality, each individual conscious self remains responsible for his subconscious soul and its content and behaviors.

The power of an uncontrolled environment, of flowing and flooding waters, wind, rain, thunder, and lightening, earthquakes and volcanoes, heat and cold, and day and night cycles, induce humans to imagine a cause. Early humans imagined a greater human-like power from which the awesome yet relative powers of the environment come from, and who can control them. Humans of the past did not draw on their intelligent ability for observation and mature logic, but on the immature imagination of childhood and adolescence. The imaginary companion of a human-like god conceived and accepted by much of the human race must be popped like a pimple, as it has protruded unsightly for far too long a time on the puerile face of humanity.

While all cannot be known, this much seems certain. Theistic religion has been built up slowly in human imagination through tradition and repeated ritual. Surely as do the retreating waves of an ocean tide, so too theistic religion will change and gradually ebb away in the great ocean of time. The western imaginary companion of a human-like god has now existed influentially for perhaps fifteen-hundred years. Yet, like children, adults must one day mature and be responsible.

John Muir (1838-1914) a Scottish-American naturalist and author, used the word god in his writings numerous times as a metaphor for the origin of the natural environment. Yet he also made a much more relevant statement. He said that the human-like god of society is "…as purely manufactured article as any puppet of a half-penny theater." By his comment, Muir suggests that a human-like god is a construct, and is conceived to make mentally apparent to humans, a first father beginning. While John Muir used the word god, he did so as a metaphor, as a word symbol of where the environment and life actually comes from, a nonhuman-like cosmological force.

Like naturalist John Muir, an individual can benefit from time spent in the environment. Exposure to the cycle of changing days and nights, odor of the earth's soil, sounds of water, winds, rains, grasses, trees, and animals, can cleanse the conscious and subconscious brain/mind to clearly see the manufactured puppet of a human-like god. Instead of a conceived and imagined human-like god, by spending time in nature an individual may become aware of the true reality of an animating soul force of life.

Soul

Many humans have faith in the unseen existence of an all-powerful human-like god who is needed to rescue the weak human soul during life and after death. Human faith and belief is much stronger in a human-like god and is much weaker in the existence of a soul. A god is thought to be immortal and not corruptible while the soul can be corrupted and is subject to punishment. In reality, a human-like god exists only as a subjective concept, as an imaginative and extreme exaggeration of human attributes, a glorified first father of humans.

In stark contrast to an imagined human-like god, a real soul does exist. Humans over emphasize an all-powerful god and underemphasize the resilient soul of life. The conceived and false over-importance of a human-like god, seeks to compensate for a real triune soul that forces life to live and to survive.

Meditations on God and the Soul

A human-like god exists only in imaginative subjective story, not in objective fact. The existence of life has not come from a first father god but instead is based on a triune soul that is a continuation of the environment, and an all-powerful cosmological force. The conscious willing effort of life is a continuation of a subconscious triune soul force of hunger for food, sex and reproduction, and aggression. The true cause of existence is not a human-like god but individual inside willing effort, supported by a mute outside environment, and an unseen and non-human-like cosmological force.

In the past, the origin of the environment and life was not perceived, and instead was desperately and wrongly misconceived to be a human-like god. While the activating soul of life has been loosely thought and spoken of as what animates life, it has not been correctly perceived and articulated and therefore it too has been wrongly misconceived. A human-like god does not make a soul, instead a triune soul is a continuation of energy of the environment and a cosmological force.

John Muir (1838-1914) naturalist and author, made the statement, "We all flow from one fountain Soul." When he used the words flow and soul, Muir must have been referring to the relative motion of the environment and growth of living forms. All is a moving and flowing continuation of a sole cosmological force, as the motion of earth, sun, moon, and stars, and the silent growth of living forms. A sole cosmological force is immanent as a triune soul force in an array of living forms.

The philosopher Baruch Spinoza (1632-1677) made the comment that "We feel and know that we are eternal." While humans may feel they are eternal at times, yet they do not really know how they are eternal. Not comprehending what the soul is, each is a stranger to each, at times alienated, dwelling in a strange land and time.

The over-estimation and fawning over an imagined human-like god, is simultaneously the under-estimation of an innate and real human soul. The subconscious soul has evolved the conscious human self that in turn has reasoned out a human-like model of a god.

The western god is then utilized as an ideational support with which to progress forward into the unknown, under the protection of a known human-like origin.

It is through not comprehending the function of the human soul that the concept of a human-like god is overvalued. The conceived and false, and at its fanatical zenith, hallucinated view of a human-like first father god has been grossly overvalued at the cost of the real triune soul. A soul is real while a human-like god is imagined and false. The human soul is a real animating force of life that resists destruction as it is a continuation of a cosmological force.

Experiencing illness, injury, ageing, and dying, many helpless humans have haphazardly concluded they cannot save themselves. Humans are vulnerable and therefore it is difficult to think of a special resilient soul inside of the frail human body. When conceived, the soul inside the body is usually thought of as passive, is thought of as being activated by and subject to reward and punishment by an all-powerful human-like god. There is also some human fear about entering into the unknown realm of death, and that the soul can be destroyed and so must be saved by what is known, a human-like god. In many religions and popular thinking, what is good and wonderful about the human soul is its ability to survive death, and is also said to be rational and to have the ability to think.

The Catholic Encyclopedia defines the human soul as "…the ultimate internal principle by which we think, feel, and will, and by which our bodies are animated." Another statement by the Encyclopedia on what the soul is suggests Catholic theologians are open to the findings of modern research on the topic. The church states that their definition of the soul is inclusive as it "…enshrines the principles of ancient speculation, and is ready to receive and assimilate the fruits of modern research." The church also favors the view that the soul at birth is rational, stating, "Many modern theologians maintain that a fully rational soul is infused into the embryo at the first moment of its existence."

I agree with the statement that the soul is the ultimate internal presence inside the body, and that the soul is what animates the body. However, unlike the church, I assert that no human-like god exists to fashion a special human soul of life that is in need of being saved. Instead, a triune soul force consists of hunger for food, sex and reproduction, and aggression.

Life is lived by the subconscious triune soul force of hunger, sex, and aggression. The soul literally forces life to survive and live. This triune soul force animates the organism to function and to action, as it is a continuation and impetus of the environment and a sole cosmological force. As a continuation of a cosmological force and the energy of a supporting environment, a triune soul force activates life, forces it to grow and move as behavior and in humans to evolve conscious willing thoughts to survive.

As for the Catholic church attitude of being "ready to receive and assimilate the fruits of modern research" on the topic of soul, this can hardly be sincere and truthful. For the church, dogma or authoritative statements are essential for its continuing existence. The church also favors the view of the human soul to be rational and capable of thinking. Yet a rational soul is an oxymoron.

The irrational subconscious soul of the body and major areas of the brain, has evolved the conscious rational thinking of the minor area of the brain. A soul is what enables life to survive. Brought into existence through reproduction, life has not much conscious choice but to subconsciously live out its allotted time by eating, having sex and reproducing, and aggressively competing.

Evolved from germ cells in the developing embryo, male sperm and female egg cells are immanent with the triune soul force as an innate effort to move, join, and grow. The motile sperm journeys to the womb where it meets the egg after it has moved down the fallopian tube. Following joining and fertilization, a journey occurs to implant on the womb membrane wall.

The subconscious triune soul is innate in this process of growth and developing life.

In the fertilized egg there is hunger for nourishment. There is a mild forerunner of aggression in attachment and implanting to the womb wall so as to obtain nourishment from the mother. Of course sex is not expressed at this early stage, only reproduction of cells and growth. Yet it has been observed that the penis develops in the male fetus between thirteen to thirty-six weeks after conception. Ultrasound photographs have also confirmed that erection of the penis occurs while in the womb. Mothers have also observed erections of their male newborns while changing diapers.

Soul Misconceptions

To compensate for the real unflattering survival traits of the human soul, hunger for food, sex and reproduction, and aggression, the Semitic cultures overvalued a human-like first father god. On the other hand, while having many human-like gods and goddesses, the more capable Hindu culture focused on comprehending the conscious self and subconscious soul through exploration of the body and brain/mind disciplines of asceticism, yoga, and meditation. Hindus also explored how through cause and effect of karma, the powerfully resilient soul continues for many lifetimes.

Through forest living and discipline of eating one meal daily, celibacy, and compassion, Buddha comprehended the soul force, yet he did not clearly say or explain what the soul is, at least as evident in recorded words attributed to him.

While excelling at exploring the brain/mind and body, Hindus misconceived the soul or atma to be good. They described the soul as having the attributes of "Sat, Chit, Ananda," meaning, true essence, pure consciousness, and bliss. This is the worst kind of error that the Hindu seer Buddha corrected. In reality, blissful essence comes from the achievement of reducing and ridding the individual of the soul. Buddha correctly focused on the problem of the soul with his teaching of anatma, or not soul. This teaching looks at the body, sensory sensations, feeling, willing, and brain/mind functions of perceptions, conceptions, picture images of now, past, and future, as not an eternal soul.

In contrast, the much more primitive Semitic cultures failed to explore brain/mind and body functions. Instead they overvalued an abstract human-like first father god. Aryan Europe, especially the southern countries followed in this harmful error. In the twenty-first century, those who favor the theistic tradition of error seek to continue it, much to their discredit and detriment to clear perception and comprehension.

Rather than seek to find the roots of life and human-kind on earth, the Semitic solution to the problem of human origin took a simple mathematical turn toward a past time. There occurred a conceptual turn along a genealogical line of previous fathers to a first father, a human-like maker of environment and all life. To a simple math calculation of one or first beginning, artistic imagination added words of story, to be displayed on the limiting mental walls of the Semitic cultural enclosure. In deference to earthly patriarchal male authority, Semitic theistic religion emphasizes a human-like first father male god.

The triune soul of life is a primary reality while a human-like god arrived only much later in a story of an imaginary first father companion. Human reason is an evolute of an unthinking soul, and is not from the reasoning of a human-like god. A triune soul forces life to function and to live as a direct continuation of the environment and a cosmological force.

Life is akin and relative as all living forms share molecular DNA, and all share a soul force that is a continuation of an unhuman-like cosmological force. A greater cosmic Go of motion is objectively real while a human-like god is only subjectively real as a conceived idea in the brain/mind.

Jesus, Soul, and God

While there exist many contradictions in the New Testament gospels, it is possible to discern three truths found by Jesus during his brief lifetime.

The statements attributed to Jesus, evidentially suggest there is an individual soul that survives physical death, and that there is an afterlife dimension. At the end of his life he also found that there is no human-like first father god.

The words of Jesus do not mention a Sheol under the earth or a sleep with the ancestors waiting passively for the body to be resurrected by a human-like god. In some way, Jesus had knowledge there is a soul that remains animated after death. Speculatively speaking, he may have been influenced by the Greek and Roman cultures, and possibly by Hindu thinking. He may also have had his own visionary experience of the afterlife in dreams and visions.

Being a good Israelite, Jesus could not transcend his culture so he kept the human-like first father god figure, the preferred cultural way of identifying the origin of existence. He retained the human-like god, yet changed the personality from a legal commandment oriented god, and retooled it to be a loving father figure. A first father figure appealed to the populace that someone cared about them enough to ease the troubles of life, and to make a place for them in an afterlife.

In reality, the loving god of Jesus is a metaphor for an afterlife that lovingly welcomes each, giving each deserved relief from the toil and turmoil of living. But the dimension is not inhabited by a human-like god. The Aramaic word Jesus used for the human-like god origin of existence is Eloi or Alaha. He also used the Aramaic word abba, meaning father. Evidence that he realized he was mistaken in the existence of a human-like first father god, occurred while being crucified. This is the poignant cry of disillusionment, and the painful truth of a mistaken metaphor revealed.

"My God, my God, why hast thou forsaken me?" (Matthew 27:46; Mark 15:34).

Curse of Limited Knowledge

In the Genesis story, the Jews whose growth of limited knowledge was symbolized by a tree, obviously saw themselves as cursed, evidently reflected in the words spoken by the artistically created word portrait of their god. The Jews thought they were cursed by their own human-like first father god. In reality, the Jews were cursed by an evolved reoccurring hunger for food every few hours and toiling to obtain it, cursed by the pleasure and pain of sex and reproduction of life, and cursed by aggression both from inside the body directed outward, and from the outside environment. They also saw themselves as cursed by physical death.

The Jews saw themselves as helpless and dependent on the imaginary companion of their first father god who formed the first human body from the earth and began the process of life by breathing into it. Reflecting the limited thinking of the Jews, their god did not create an immortal soul within. Therefore, the human body is in a sense also cursed by a lack of a soul, as nothing within the body survived physical death. The body was formed from the earth to which it returned when breathing stopped. The shadow/shade of the individual then entered the pit of Sheol and joined with the darkness under the earth. A later Jewish theological upgrade of thinking consisted of burial and a "dirt nap" of sleep, and a passive waiting for the human-like god to resurrect the body. For the Jews, death and not having a soul was compensated for by having a long lifespan on the earth. (Genesis 5)

Thinking ability of the Middle East cultures during the time of Jesus, was poor, and much less skilled than that of Greek and Hindu philosophy. For the Jews, the only way to survive physical death was reassembly of the physical body. The culture has been and continues to be stuck with this paltry way of thinking. The afterlife dimension mentioned by Jesus is not in Sheol or in a dirt nap sleep passively awaiting resurrection from a god. He mentioned his metaphorical father's afterlife dimension many times.

"In my father's house are many mansions: if it were not so, I would have told you." (John 14:2)

"Jesus answered, My kingdom is not of this world: if my kingdom were of this world, then would my servants fight, that I should not be delivered to the Jews: but now is my kingdom not from hence." (John 18:36)

The gospel, or good news of Jesus was better than the old news of the Jews. The ability to enter and exist in an afterlife is inside of each individual, with the caveat of, as long as the person is good. The northern fatherly god of Jesus was loving and comforted the good, yet he also burned the evil like sticks or weeds in the fire of Gehenna. (Matthew 13: 30; John 15:6)

The southern Judahite god emphasized many commandments, temple worship, and the resurrection of the body. The northern Israelite god of Jesus was portrayed as fatherly, and only two commandments were given to obey in the mundane setting of daily life. The individual also had an unmentioned immanent soul that upon the time of physical death entered into an afterlife beyond the earth, without waiting for a human-like god to act.

In the earliest version of the gospel of Mark, as written circa 350 CE, in the Sinaiticus gospel, there is no mention of a resurrection of Jesus. In the early gospel, chapter 16 contains only eight verses while later versions of the gospel contain an additional twelve verses that include the resurrection. The resurrection was undoubtedly added to the last chapter of the gospel of Mark by nefarious and unscrupulous monkish scribes. Since there is no mention of a physical resurrection in the earliest written gospel, there can be little importance to the notion.

The resurrection did become important and was mentioned in some of the collected works of New Testament writers who sought to fit the event within the established way of Jewish thinking. With the physical resurrection of Jesus added, it appears that his message of immediate entry into an afterlife dimension was perverted. The resurrection of the physical body conflicts with the message of Jesus that his kingdom is not of this earth, which includes a biologically dependent body.

Based on the circa 350 CE Sinaiticus gospel of Mark that does not include a mention of resurrection, Jesus seems to have directly entered an afterlife dimension. However, the various writers insist on the resurrection of the body of Jesus, and that the physical body actually entered into a dimensional afterlife.

In the later gospel of Luke 24:51 and Acts 1:1-9, Jesus left earth in his resurrected physical body. All other Jews continue to endure a long wait for their personal body resurrection. Jesus came to save the Jews from the underground pit of Sheol, and sleeping under the earth until resurrection, by announcing an afterlife dimension. His words were primarily delivered to the northern Israelites, and secondarily to the southern Judahites.

"But he answered and said, I am not sent but unto the lost sheep of the house of Israel." (Matthew 15:24)

Soul Teachings

The soul is nonexistent in the early theistic thinking of Judaism. The Jews wrote only of a shade or shadow of the body that following death entered the darkness of Sheol under the earth. Eventually, the northern Israelite by the name of Jesus of Nazareth seems to have changed this view. The words attributed to him suggest that humans have a soul that survives death, and yet following his culture, only in relation to a first father figure. The survival of the soul in an afterlife dimension became an emphasis in the "good news" of Jesus, the founder of Christianity.

The prophet Muhammad (circa 570-632 CE) brought the religion of Islam and an emphasis on surrender of personal willing to the greater willing of the god Allah. Allah will resurrect and judge each individual soul. Obedience to the omnipotent god is mandatory and the dependent soul answers to the god. In contrast with later prudish Christian teachings, Islam is more authentic in accommodating expression of the soul (nafs or rooh) and allows for sex through polygamy (up to four wives) and accommodates aggression (jihad).

Hinduism has emphasized the reality of the soul or atma but also diluted the reality of the soul with many artistically imagined gods and goddesses. Buddha did away with the faulty Hindu conception of the atma with his teaching of anatma, and he rejected the objective reality of the gods. Buddha awoke to the dynamic of how a human-like god is conceived and constructed in the brain, therefore Buddhism is a wise atheistic religion. The Chinese recognize an afterlife where the soul (hun or po) of ancestors dwell, yet the religion of Taoism also emphasizes a cosmic energy or chi, and yin-yang immanent in the individual and the environment.

The American religion of Spiritualism came along in the mid-1800s. What is important in Spiritualism is the reality of the soul, referred to as a spirit. In Spiritualism, emphasis is on the reality and survival of the soul as proven by evidential and convincing messages and communication from deceased relatives or friends received by mediums during readings. Spiritualists do not attempt to provide convincing evidence for the existence of a human-like god as evidence for it is completely lacking. For the existence of a human-like god there exists only dogma, faith, belief, and tradition. Only the idea of a human-like god and empty words to describe it are served up again and again, ad nauseum.

Free Will

The unthinking subconscious soul is prominent in eighty-one percent of the brain neurons and the entire body. To think and reason and to get along with others, the individual is guided by the limited conscious cerebral self, comprising a mere nineteen percent of total brain neurons. Based on physiology, it is convincingly evident that humans are more irrational than they are rational. In addition, if a person is under-educated, errors in judgment, poor and faulty choices, and struggle and suffering is usually the result.

Realizing life is limited, an imagined greater intelligence of a first father god who will make better choices to guide the individual, is readily accepted by the under intelligent.

Life is frustrating, and for the average person, utilizing the imagined concept of a human-like god is an easy way to transcend and to find relief from the limitations of life. A way of obtaining relief from the many limitations of existence, is by looking to the beginning and ending of it, where of course many humans station a human-like god.

The sense of human free will, is only the ability and tendency in any life situation to exert too much or not enough effort. This is what humans are free to do and not much else. Humans are only free from moment to moment to attempt the precarious balance of life with relationships, health, finances, and possessions. Life is at a minimum, the fragile potential to be in or out of balance at any point in time, caused by both outside and inside conditions, and by not enough or too much willing effort.

Experiences of personal perturbation lead many to seek assistance to maintain balance. It is quite ingrained for many during challenging situations to think not in terms of cause and effect but to think of a human-like god for assistance. In life situations, many humans spontaneously think they are being rewarded or punished by a human-god; or if not by a good god, then an evil entity. Humans imagine and utilize a human-like god to delimit their personal limitations of living.

Since the subconscious human soul only directs humans to survive, the reasoning cerebral cortex needs reinforcement. The human conscious self requires a god of good qualities to influence, control, and direct humans to what is better. A human-like god is a way of identifying and locating goodness in a particular place. Yet for humans in a limiting time sequence of past, present, and future, it is often difficult to discern what is good and what is bad. A Chinese Confucian story illustrates this difficulty quite well.

"Long ago in China, a farmer woke up early and went to get his horse to do spring plowing. To his surprise, the horse had run away. The farmer then went to one of his two neighbors and told him what had happened, and that he would have to go to town and spend money to buy another horse.

This would delay planting of his crops. His neighbor commented, "That is really bad." The farmer then went to his other neighbor to whom he then told about the runaway horse and having to spend money, and the neighbor commented, "Who knows what's good and who knows what's bad." The farmer got up early a few days later to make a journey to buy another horse. He heard a noise outside, and to his surprise looked to find his horse had returned and had brought several other wild horses. The farmer quickly closed the gate on the corral. The farmer then hastened to tell his neighbor that his horse had returned, and that now he could plow his fields, and have spare horses to use and to sell the others for a profit. His neighbor said, "That is really good!" The farmer then informed his other neighbor, to which he responded, "Who knows what's good and who knows what's bad." A few weeks later, the farmer's son attempted to ride one of the wild horses but was thrown off and broke his leg in the fall.

The farmer went to his neighbor and told him he would be shorthanded without his son and he would have to hire someone to help him with his farm chores. His neighbor commented, "That is really bad." The farmer told his other neighbor what had happened, and his neighbor said, "Who knows what's good and who knows what's bad." A month later, soldiers came to the farm, conscripting young men to fight in a war. Yet they could not take the farmer's son as he had a broken leg. The farmer told his neighbor who said, "That is really good." The farmer also told his other neighbor who said, "Who knows what is good and who knows what is bad."

For theistic oriented individuals, an imagined human-like god furnishes direction away from an unsavory and confusing earthly life toward a certainty of what is good and has good qualities. Lacking a real human model of good, then an imaginary human-like model must suffice. A god has qualities humans would like to have, such as increased strength and an ability to know more.

Humans do have some noble ideas and traits but the question asked is, where did they obtain these few good qualities? For theists, a human-like first father god is said to be endowed with exalted and perfect qualities and traits.

Therefore, a god is thought to be where the few good qualities that humans do possess have come from. In reality, humans mentally distilled any finer noble traits and qualities from themselves and attributed them to a human-like exceptionally good first father god dwelling in undisturbed repose, removed from the toil, turmoil, and carnage of daily life on the earth.

Humans see faint glimmers of good within themselves, yet the subconscious soul of life corrupts finer sensibilities. A god is an imaginary model of human self judgment that condemns the overall human qualities of human biology, behaviors, and knowledge. The subconscious soul is a barrier to any lofty godly aspiration. The soul is observed to sinfully hunger for food, for sex and reproduction, and for aggression.

In reality, the only cure for the human condition is not to project an imaginary human-like god that excels in good qualities for humans to fail in comparison. The remedy for humans is to conduct a self and soul meditative examination. When a patient presents with symptoms of illness, a good physician conducts an exam. Therefore, a responsible individual when presenting with a host of the many challenges and problems of life, will conduct a self and soul examination.

Seekers

Lay theists often attend prayer retreats for a few days or weeks. Theistic monks separate from family, friends, and the population for years to seek for a human-like god. In reality, both groups are wasting their time as they are pursuing only a conceived imaginary companion, a numerical first father of humans.

The main and necessary disciplines of religious asceticism and monasticism consist of restriction of food consumption, celibacy, and reduction of aggression by practicing tolerance and cooperation.

This disciplined effort is often directed to please and to receive a response from a human-like god but in reality is a direct encounter with the powerful triune soul that forces life to live. Searching for a human-like god is to go in a false direction, to arrive only at an imaginary companion.

Moses spent time on a desert mountain. Rather than conduct an internal self and soul examination, Moses' is said to have been given law commandments by an external human-like god with which to enforce and maintain social order. The interaction with an imaginary companion is a poor superficial substitute for self and soul knowledge.

Jesus retreated into the countryside where he is portrayed as encountering the evil tempter Satan who opposes a human-like god. In reality, the encounter is with the triune soul that forces life to live. Hunger for food produced the temptation of turning stones into bread. If Jesus bowed down, he was offered to rule over all the many kingdoms, and this would have necessitated aggression to maintain the rule. Sex and reproduction is not mentioned as a temptation. Instead, Jesus is asked to jump down from Herod's temple, and if he is the son of a god, then angels will protect him from the fall. Since a human-like god is an imaginary companion, Jesus wisely replied that one should not tempt or test the first father god as the efficacy would be nil.

Following in the theistic tradition, Muhammad, the founder of Islam, did not investigate the conscious self and the subconscious soul. After spending some time of deprivation in a small cave, he was joined by the imaginary companion of an angel who then and later over a time of twenty years, conveyed to him only abstract words that became the loose arrangement of the Quran.

Only the wonderfully wise man known as the Buddha managed to find what is true about the soul and a human-like god. He retreated to the forest to reduce distractions of the senses, especially sights and sounds. In the natural quiet of the forest he closed his eyes and removed attention from outside sensations. He then focused on inside sensations of breathing.

Meditatively focusing on sensations of breathing, he noticed picture images intruding and distracting attention. Turning attention, he then began to observe the visual picture making of thoughts, as images of now, past, and future. Calming the picture making process, he began to observe and to encounter the body and the triune soul that forces life to live, as hunger for food, sex and reproduction, and aggression. The soul and not a human-like god is what originates and forces life to live again and again. This internal struggle with the soul is portrayed as a story in which Buddha underwent the privation of fasting from food. He also successively neutralized aggressive attacks from Mara the evil one and his alluring daughters who attempted to seduce him. (The Book of Kindred Sayings, The Mara Suttas)

Content of Consciousness

The content of human conscious awareness consists of the following:

1. Sensations of the senses.
2. Brain picture images of now, past, and future.
3. Conscious brain willing of the voluntary central nervous system.
4. Body willing of the subconscious triune soul force for food, sex and reproduction, and aggression, expressed as cell and organ function and behavior.

The failure to distinguish and sort through these conglomerate yet distinct cognitive functions is what Buddha referred to when he spoke of ignorance (avidya). These processes are also what Hindus refer to as maya, illusion of the senses and delusion of ideas. In western theism the failure to sort through these processes causes sin, separation from individual wholeness, imagined to be the holiness of a human-like god. This is the circular subject-object loop of experience that must be meditatively observed, examined, sorted out and comprehended by observing the content of the brain/mind, and the parts and functions of the body.

The individual must meditatively explore the conscious self and the subconscious soul. In meditation there are four areas of brain and body activity that must be relaxed and reduced.

1. Reduce attention to sensations of the senses by closing the eyes in a quiet place.
2. Focus on an internal sensation such as breathing.
3. Reduce conscious picture images of now moments, memory, and future images.
4. Reduce subconscious willing of the triune soul force of hunger for food, sex and reproduction, and aggression.

Sensations of the senses continuously change. There is a continual stream of sensations through and from the senses to the brain where they are subconsciously transformed and consciously perceived as picture images. Brain neurons transform changing sensory sensations into images of now moments, memory, and images of an imagined future that guide willing responses of body behavior. Meditative attention observes there are now sensations, there are picture images, and there are willing intentions that lead to behaviors. A meditative focus of attention observes an impermanence of sensation; observes an impermanence of picture images, and observes an impermanence of both brain and body willing as intentions for food, sex and reproduction, and aggression.

Willing is the primary reality of brain and body and is guided by knowing picture images constructed from sensations. Willing in a single cell organism is guided by sensations or stimuli as there is a lack of picture images. Visually impaired or blind individuals are guided by and base their willing behavior on sensations of sound. Sensations from both the inside and outside guide the organism's willing effort to obtain nourishment, have sex or reproduce, and exert aggression.

Meditation is a focus of attention and intention for the purpose of observation. During meditation, attention is removed from sensations outside of the body to observation of sensations inside the body.

With consistent practice, the meditator also comes to notice the stream of visual images that divert attention from sensations of immediate moments, to memory and future. Meditatively reducing and stilling the flow of picture images and not falling asleep, cognitive processes can be better observed.

Meditation slows remembering and imagining, slows breathing and relaxes the body, not to sleep but to be more conscious of subconscious images stored in the brain and sensing of subconscious functioning of the body. Meditation is an exploration of conscious behavior and subconscious willing of cells and organs. Both conscious and subconscious repeated willing behaviors become entangled with picture images organized and filed in a time sequence of now, past, and future. Meditative observation can sort through and separate the tangled conflation of willing effort with brain/mind images. In this way, clarity of attention is attained, and an awakening from the sleep of individual habits of thoughts and behaviors.

The average person busy with family, friends, and work, observes predominantly what is outside until physical or emotional pain directs attention inside the body. In contrast, wisdom reserves time to observe inside brain/mind and body functions, to focus attention, to ponder, muse, and to meditate. Those who meditate acquire wisdom, live healthy, learn much, and who know how to make, save, and spend money. Time spent with the wise and learned is uplifting, while time spent with fools and the unlearned is a waste of time and an unnecessary burden.

Meditation requires effort and must be practiced consistently so as to best sort out the human self and soul. Usually any effort at introspection and meditation results in vacant attention, distraction, and sleep. Yet practice may eventually lead to a steady focus of attention and discernment of the cognitive process of god-making, and to clearly distinguishing self and soul functions.

Subject-Object

The image of an outside object is formed inside the brain of a subject. For a meditator, this process merits attention and investigation. Object images of now, past, and future, are perceptual constructions that serve subjective willing and behaviors. The subconscious perceptual construct of a conscious picture image inside is constructed from sensations of an outside object. Sensations from outside are subconsciously formed into images inside, to appear in conscious awareness.

Meditation is the practice of sorting through the conscious and mostly subconscious processing of the picture images that pair the subject with an object. Meditative attention inspects the sensate process of picture images stored as memories that when recalled are held by attention to guide the person in daily now activities. Conscious attention reduces continual changing picture images of objects and a meditator becomes content with much less content. With conscious conceptual associative thinking reduced, both conscious attention and subconscious perception are enhanced.

An object appears in the brain of the subject. The subject brain then wills for or against the object and responds with behavior, or may activate knowledge and reflect on the object. Brain willing and knowing mutually activate each other. Individual brain and body willing for or against of the conscious self and subconscious soul, is a continuation of a nonlocal cosmological force, field, or ground.

Attention

Now moments are tenuous and fleeting, supported by memory of past experiences, and by imagined possible or probable future events. The origin of conscious attention has evolved from the subconscious function of the body. The body begins as the subconscious function of sperm and egg to form an embryo that develops into a fetus and a newborn.

The moving force of life to function, is the triune soul. The triune soul is longer lasting than is the body, and as a continuation of a cosmological force, is resistant to destruction.

Fleeting change of conscious attention is supported by the habit ladened, longer lasting subconscious function of the body. Both the body and the triune soul force are a continuation of the longer lasting non-conscious energy elements of the environment that are a continuation of an everlasting cosmological force or ground.

A human subject cannot sense a cosmological force to be an object. This is where human reason fabricates and applies a patch to the unknown, to be a known human-like numerical first father god. If more individuals were meditatively aware of their cognitive processes, they would observe how attention switches from now moments to imagining a human-like god. There would then be no habitual belief or theistic tradition.

Shadow and Soul

A theistic god is a conceived abstract idea, a way of focusing on the origin of existence, an arbitrary inserted first father in the sequence of many forefathers and descendant fathers. The first father god of Genesis formed the first human from the soil of the earth and called him Adamah, meaning, red earthling. The first human is said to be made from the dust, the red soil of the earth, probably the mineral red ochre.

The god breathed into the man and he became a nephesh, a Hebrew word meaning, a living breathing creature. There was no soul in the man, nothing that insured survival. When an Old Testament person died, there occurred only a natural transition of the individual human "shade or shadow" reflected on the surface of the earth, to go down under to join the ever-dark pit of Sheol. Having an overemphasis on the first father god of the generations, the soul was pitifully not conceived by the Jews. To say that what remained of the physical body was the shade or shadow of the individual that joined with the darkness under the earth, is a primitive conception.

The Jews portrayed the origin of existence to be a human-like god who molded the first man from the red soil of the earth, and animated him to life by breathing into him.

Breathing just got life going and nothing special was transferred from the god to the human. Breathing while vital for life, is just breathing, it is a natural not a supernatural process.

The animating force of a human-like god remains outside of the body. The god is said to shape the body from outside and only got it to live by applying an early form of mouth-to-mouth cardiopulmonary resuscitation (CPR). Conceiving of the vital animating force of life remaining outside of the mortal breathing body, Jews are totally dependent on their projected imaginary companion of an all-powerful human-like god. At the time of death, the deceased Jew can only wait in sleep to be revived during a time and day of future resurrection. It is an imaginative fairy tale that the animating force is a human-like god located outside of the human body. In reality, the animating force is inside of the body as a triune soul that is a continuation of a cosmological force.

Most likely influenced by Greek and/or Hindu teachings on the soul, a northern Israelite by the name of Jesus attempted to correct the existential ignorance of the Jews who conceived humans to have only a shade or shadow, and did not have a soul. He corrected the Semitic view that relied exclusively on a human-like god instead of an animating soul that survived death and entered into an afterlife. Jesus unfortunately also continued to be influenced by tradition and continued to refer to a human-like first father god as well. The soul continues to be underemphasized by Jews, Christians, and Muslims, who overemphasize an all-powerful first father god. The god is needed to save the weak individual from oblivion, and to either reward or punish the helpless and dependent human.

There is no real human-like god. What is real is the triune soul within that is a continuation of an all-powerful cosmological force. What saves an individual during life and an afterlife is not a god but an all-powerful triune soul force of hunger for food, sex and reproduction, and aggression. An all-powerful Christian triune god is a subjectively conceived idea for an objective cosmological force. The Christian triune god is also a projection of the metaphysical reality of a triune soul inside the physical body.

Theistic religion considers human character to be dishonest, prone to conflict with others, potentially criminal and violent, and afflicted with a guilty conscience. Theistic religion sees the human soul as convoluted and contaminated with separating sin from an immortal and ideal human-like god. Since objective relief is often lacking in life, humans turn away from reality and accept the subjective belief of an imaginary human-like god. In reality, the reward after death is not coexistence with a human-like god but is a relief from life, and entry into an afterlife dimension.

Resurrection

Middle East populations and religions, have to wishfully imagine a resurrection of the body as they cannot perceive and did not conceive of a soul. There is only the physical body and not a metaphysical soul. It remains to be seen whether a human-like god can put all the human parts that once broken from accident, aggression or age, back together again. In reality, the task of resurrecting a human body and reassembling its parts by an imaginary first father god, will turn out similar to results in the fairy tale of Humpty Dumpty.

In the thinking of Middle East religions, there is nothing inside the body that could separate and survive physical death. There is only the life (nephesh) of the body. There is no immediate spontaneous rising of the soul following death but a raising or resurrecting of the physical body in a long future time by a human-like god. The physical dead body will have to wait until it will be raised on the Day of Judgment. This scenario disrespects human dignity and portrays them as completely dependent on a human-like god. This is an obvious case of metaphysical immaturity and patriarchal worship by the members of Judaism, Christianity, and Islam. These three religions are exclusively patriarchal as they each worship a human-like first father god.

The miraculous maker of life conceived to be a human-like god is looked to restore the remains of a dead body to life. This clung to delusion of a human-like outside animator, overlooks what truly animates the body on the inside, a soul.

The notion of waiting for a resurrection, removes the importance of a soul that can survive physical death on its own, by its own innate property of what it is, a continuation of a cosmological force. The importance of the resurrection is a glorifying of a human-like first father god's ability to raise the dead and reassemble the body. There is no mention of a soul's ability to survive on its own. An immortal soul has no need of a human-like god. In the religion of Hinduism, and especially Buddhism, no god is required, the soul or karma of the person reincarnates on its own.

There are Christians who want their body saved and resurrected, and there are those who want the essence of the body saved, the soul. The primitive notion of resurrection is evident even in the bodily ascension of Jesus into an afterlife. The nephesh or life of his actual physical living body, we are told, ascended to a heaven afterlife dimension.

"Behold my hands and my feet, that it is I myself: handle me, and see; for a spirit hath not flesh and bones, as ye see me have." Luke 24:39 "And it came to pass while he blessed them, he parted from them, and was carried up into heaven." (Luke 24: 51)

The notion of a human-like god has many subjective meanings but no objective reality. Since a human-like first father god does not exist in reality, the Last Judgment spoken of by theistic religions will therefore not occur. Like the theistic tenet of a human-like god, the last judgment is also a metaphor or allegory. Yet to what subjective reality experience, if any, does it allude to? The subjective reality of the last judgment is that it instills both fear of punishment and hopes of reward. It projects individual conscience to the concept of a human-like god outside, to be shared by many. In reality, after physical death, there may occur a subjective individual judgment of whether to proceed to better dimensions or to reincarnate and live on earth again.

While a human soul is thought to be special, this specialness does not come from a human-like god. What is special about the soul, is that it resists destruction and may not be able to be destroyed.

Soul Survival

It has been long generally accepted humans have a soul that survives death but as to what the soul is, has not been well investigated and known. Based on what is known of brain function, it can be speculated and extrapolated that the percentage of the soul that contributes to survival is greater while the percentage of the soul that thinks and reasons is minimal. Extrapolating from biological life, the soul only partially thinks and reasons.

The field of modern neuroscience estimates that the human brain consists of eighty-six billion neurons. Of this total number the cerebral cortex consists of sixteen billion neurons and is the predominant reasoning area of the brain. In contrast, the part of the brain known as the cerebellum regulates body movement and consists of sixty-nine billion neurons. The midbrain regulates the subconscious autonomic sympathetic and parasympathetic nervous system of the body and consists of roughly one billion neurons. The total for non-cerebral and non-reasoning neurons of the brain consists of approximately seventy billion.

Of the total eighty-six billion brain neurons, a minority sixteen billion or nineteen percent are possibly utilized for reasoning, and the other majority seventy billion or eighty-one percent regulate one hundred trillion cells of the body. Four times more brain neurons regulate body functions than are utilized for reasoning. The subconscious triune soul force of hunger for food, sex and reproduction, and aggression, is immanent in one hundred trillion cells of the body and autonomic nervous system, cerebellum and midbrain. The triune soul supports and easily overwhelms conscious reasoning of the cerebral cortex.

Neuroscience further estimates that of the brain's cerebral cortex that consists of sixteen billion neurons, only from one percent to ten percent (one hundred million to one billion six hundred thousand) cells are consciously aware at any particular waking moment. The ability to reason and to be aware in any given moment is limited.

Most human problems of life are caused by an inadequate reasoning ability, and by the triune soul. Hunger for food is always a problem as it must be obtained and consumed on an average of every four hours. Many problems come from sex and reproduction. Aggression is always ready to obtain or defend. The triune soul functions of the body are expressed as three main physical systems:

    Digestive
    Genital
    Muscles

There are traditional ways of disciplining these three systems of the body and triune soul. Full or mild celibacy is the individual denial to participate in the sex act and reproduction of life. Celibacy is the personal effort to proclaim "no" to life, and is a traditional way of avoiding conflict, toil, and caring for life. The strong individual urge and tension for sex and reproduction, is a direct continuation of an outside cosmological force that brings the environment and living forms into existence.

The practice of pacifism or nonviolence is the determination not to participate in aggression. Veganism is the dietary practice of not harming and consuming sentient living forms. Fasting from food is the individual determination to confront and to control the life force of the physical body.

Reincarnation

Humans are fearful of a dead body, not only due to the eventual decay and stench but also the possible spread of the contagion of death to the living. Humans also vaguely and dimly sense that the body when living consists of energy and force that can continue to exist as a soul or ghost.

When a person dies, humans observe and ponder about the dead body and its parts, and on what previously moved it that is no longer inside. Does what moves the body terminate in oblivion with its demise and decay?

Humans have long marveled about what if anything leaves the body at the time of death. Something not visible seems to be missing as the body no longer moves. What is missing in the body, is that there is no longer a subconscious and conscious willing for food, sex and reproduction, and aggression. When the triune soul force departs, the body no longer moves and functions.

The soul is an ambivalent cluster of surviving force, as is popularly said consisting of "love and hate," alluding to the triune force of sex and reproduction and aggression, both supported by hunger for food. The cluster has come into existence and is composed of relative energy and force that both causes and endures change. Life is forced to live by a triune soul, a continuation of the relative energy elements of the environment that in turn is a continuation of cosmological force.

When the mostly subconscious habit laden soul force leaves the body, it is conserved by what are called the "laws of conservation," of energy, mass, and momentum. The triune soul is also conserved dimensionally by quantum entanglement or interconnectedness, and is resistant to destruction as it is a continuation of a cosmological force, field, or ground.

In many individual case studies, psychoanalysts have convincingly shown that forgotten unconscious memories of childhood continue to exist, and unless resolved, exert an unconscious influence on conscious personality over a lifetime. This capacity also seems to extend from one lifetime to another future lifetime. There is a saying, "Where there is a will, there is a way." I would have to agree with this statement. For as long as there is conscious and subconscious willing of the triune soul for food, sex and reproduction, and aggression, there will be a way for it to be expressed. As a continuation of a cosmological force, the relative triune soul is the cosmological animating fuel of life. The willing triune effort of life is a continuation of a cosmological force that moves the universe into existence, and as a continuation of this process, the triune soul is resistant to destruction.

There exist many case studies conducted by Dr. Ian Stevenson, Dr. Brian Weiss, and others. The research suggests that wanting to continue, a minimally conscious and predominant subconscious willful soul, can join with the cells of a developing embryo or fetus.

Numerous case studies suggest that regardless of genetic traits of parents and family members, a cluster of conserved subconscious willing efforts may through affinity, seek a body to continue to will again. The word affinity is defined as, "An attraction or force between particles that cause them to combine." A surviving cluster of human willing may through affinity seek a new life and to have a biological body again.

For the will to live, all is acceptable. For the triune soul, what is important is to continue; this is its primary function and only goal in time. Particular events may be stored as memory, and the soul as a continuation of a cosmological force, may want to subconsciously retain or repeat them for a better or worse life.

Ocean of Time

The heritage of life is connected to the ocean, a vestige of which continues to exist in the body today. Living forms also dwell on a solid earth that in reality is a sea of energy, composed of atoms and electrons of the elements.

Whether coming from somewhere in space to the planet, or originating on earth, life was first nurtured in quiet tidal edges of the ever changing ocean. Life mimics the sea to repeat an ageless pattern of moving, flowing, and change. Humans behave like waves of fluid change that struggle night and day to advance with excitement, and to retreat from the ennui of a stable shore. Each individual soul mimics the sea by ever reaching for and soon relinquishing its hold on stability, in the ebb and flow of life and death.

The unseen animating force of moon gravity pulls and pushes the restless energy particles of water together to form waves.

Meditations on God and the Soul

The ocean waves rhythmically advance yet must retreat and then return to crash some more; senseless spectacle but exhilarating. Such is life as well.

Both the solid earth and liquid waters are continually in motion and change. Beyond limited sensory reality of appearance, both earth and water consist of radiant energy of elements, atoms, and electrons, and quantum particles. These are a continuation of relative strong and weak nuclear force, magnetism, and gravity forces that in turn are a continuation of a cosmological force or ground.

Not a human-like god but impersonal time, the progression of change, brings both reward and ruin to environment and life alike. Beginningless and endless, forever and ever, is the moving force of change both in the outside environment, and as a continuation inside living forms. From an un-ageing cosmological force comes all ageing environmental and living forms. What moves as an activating force in human subconscious function of cells and organs, and conscious willing and knowing, is the will to live of the triune soul of hunger for food, sex and reproduction, and aggression.

Time is transformation, change from one relative condition to another, and the true lord is not a human-like god but that which moves life, the triune soul as a continuation of the environment and a cosmological force.

Faulty Knowledge

The natural environment has evolved humans to experience four primary kinds of intense satisfaction and fulfillment. These four are eating of food, sexual orgasm, aggression, and learning. The two major functions of the brain are the primary cerebellum and midbrain of the subconscious autonomic nervous system, and the secondary cerebral cortex of the conscious central nervous system. The primary and major function of the midbrain consists of the rewarding orgasmic satisfaction of having sex and reproduction, eating food, and use of aggression.

The secondary evolved cerebral brain function, is the satisfying fulfillment of learning, and the mildly orgasmic "aha" moments of comprehension and knowledge.

Not until the twentieth century has the theory and evidence of evolution been accepted. Humans have only recently begun to think of species as evolving from lower to higher intelligence. A mere glance at history and fossil evidence is convincing for evolution.

Traditionally, theistic religions have long held the view of having been made by and having failed a higher god intelligence. To express where the evolved ability for learning and knowledge has come from, some small portion of the population has artistically imagined and erected a mental word built sculpture of a human-like god. The greater portion of the earth's population have uncritically accepted this childish conception of an imaginary companion.

In the biblical Genesis story, the first father god endowed the first humans with a basic knowledge of how to live. He even brought the animals to Adam to see what he would name them (Genesis 2:19-20). This early lower level of good knowledge caused no trouble for the god or the first humans. The basic innate human knowledge endowed by the first father god was good.

But oh no! It seems the god had a store of additional knowledge that he deliberately kept from humans. The god placed some of his own godly knowledge in a special tree where in time it bore fruit. Of course human taste buds naturally like sweet fruits, and despite being warned, the first humans soon consumed the forbidden fruit. The fruit obtained from the mythic Tree of Knowledge of Good and Evil is symbolic of experience. Fruits grow and ripen and then deteriorate in time. If other life forms do not consume them, fruits drop to the ground and rot. Following death the human body also rots away.

The knowledge that the first humans obtained was the knowledge of nudity, sex and reproduction, and death. (Genesis 3:7; 4:1-2)

The scenario begs a question, what did the god previously do with this kind of knowledge? Since the god has this knowledge, did he previously have sex with another god, goddess, or human? In the Jewish tale, unlike the basic knowledge bestowed by the god, the secondary acquired knowledge from the tree fruit was troublesome to both the god and to the first two, and eventually all later humans. In reality, the acquired secondary knowledge stage is an evolving and increasing conscious self-knowledge, and a faint yet faulty conscious knowledge of the subconscious triune soul.

Vaguely sensing but not recognizing the significance of the human soul, Jews lacked the contemplative ability to further investigate, or intentionally shrank from the daunting challenge. Instead, the Jews placed their hope on an imaginary companion, a human-like first father god who condemned and cursed human life. The curse directed by the god toward human life, is a story distortion and condemnation of the reality that life contains an unrecognized innate triune soul force. Not clearly seeing this, the Hebrews/Jews saw the body as returning to dust, and the shade or shadow of a person entering the dark of Sheol under the earth.

The Genesis story of the bible tells how a human-like god made an exclusive and pleasurable Garden of Eden for the first humans. He created them non-sexually and also provided sustenance. There was no pain of hunger, no sex and reproduction, and no aggression. Only from human disobedience did the experience of pain come into existence through obtaining the knowledge of both good and evil.

The god made and stored at least some of his knowledge in the fruits of a special tree. The god-made knowledge acquired by humans, is portrayed to have occurred all at once during a fruit-tasting event. In reality, human acquired trial and error knowledge that dawned and evolved slowly over many thousands of years. The special fruit taken from the Tree of Knowledge of Good and Evil represents increasing and evolving human comprehension of a fragile existential life.

The human-like god of Genesis created humans with only a basic good knowledge. The fruit from the Tree of Knowledge of Good and Evil is the mechanism of how both good and evil knowledge got into humans. The story relates that the god is not to be faulted for placing both good and evil knowledge inside a special fruit. By consuming the fruit, humans are instead faulted for placing both good and evil knowledge inside of themselves. Since the Jewish god could not be portrayed as directly endowing humans with good and evil knowledge, the solution was that the god had to be portrayed as placing his faulty good and evil knowledge in the fruit of a special tree. In reality, the concept of a human-like god that is not at fault, is a faulty story.

Some mechanism had to be devised as the god could not be portrayed as creating or enabling humans to acquire evil knowledge. Humans had to be portrayed at fault by placing evil knowledge inside of their own bodies and brain.

Since little wisdom is to be had in life, especially in the cultures of the Middle East, the Jewish god is not portrayed as being especially smart nor wise. Since the god was low on wisdom, no Tree of Wisdom was made and placed in the Garden of Eden. There was only a tree of faulty good and evil knowledge, made by the faulty Jewish conceived imagining of a human-like first father god.

Three episodes occurred in the Garden of Eden that reveal the specific knowledge acquired by humans. The act of eating the fruit is knowledge of a concern for hunger; knowledge of nudity and sex brought about the begetting of offspring; knowledge of aggression between the two brothers Cain and Abel, brought the first death to humankind.

Where did a god of goodness obtain the knowledge of nudity, sex, and reproduction? Of course it was meant for humans to have the knowledge of how life is in reality. Life is not all good, it is composed of at least half evil experiences. At this point the contrived Garden scenario begs a question. How much better can a human-like first father god's heavenly house be when his created life and earthly dwelling is of such poor construction?

In the Genesis tale, the god pronounced that all he had made was good, and even very good. (Chapter 1) Yet suddenly, a serpent appeared (Chapter 2) as a symbol of the "not good" the god had made but who the god had not previously mentioned. Rather than the humanlike god who set up existence, the serpent became the contributing cause of human deception and acquiring faulty knowledge. Existence often looks safe and benign but like the serpent is deceptive. Recurring cycles of accidents, disease, weather catastrophes, crimes, and war are always prevalent.

Since it was posited that life is good and pleasurable when first made, something must have happened to change existence from completely good, to both good and evil. To find an explanation, human attention was directed back through time toward the premier ancestor, the first father of existence who created them. Yet in the Genesis story, blame for a faulty existence was not given to the first father god but to the first humans. The biblical patriarchal authors placed blame not on the first father but on the importance of human knowing and willing. The blame for a good and evil life bestowed on humans, vaguely alludes to but does not reveal the true cause of life.

The authors of the Garden of Eden story had to have felt hesitant, ambivalent, and guilty about blaming the originating first father for the long sequence of human suffering. Instead, personal guilt was assumed and conceived to be a particular human act of disobedience in relation to a patriarchal first father. The blamed incident was the obtaining of increased knowledge of life that caused strife and conflict with the environment and among humans.

Since it was observed humans have daily knowledge of hunger for food, sex and reproduction, and aggression, they must have obtained it from some place and at some time in the past. Surely the superior knowledge of a god could not and would not develop an inferior faulty human product. Faulty knowledge and behavior could only be that of inferior humans.

Rather than a first father human-like god being guilty of a challenging life existence, it was human knowledge acquired during a portrayed single act of disobedience that was the cause of the many generational human struggle, pain, and sufferings of life.

Obviously the godly knowledge obtained was not how to create human life using thoughts and words, as did the human-like god. The knowledge obtained from the Tree of Knowledge of Good and Evil was of body nudity that led to sex and physical reproduction. In reality, the Garden of Eden tale is a human lament on the limitation of inferior conscious human knowledge, and the dominance of the subconscious soul. The Genesis story of faulty and inferior, yet god made knowledge acquired by humans, is a lament that the human soul consists of a triune force of hunger for food, sex and reproduction, and aggression.

In reality, the tale relates through dumb allegory, how the rational cerebral cortex of the brain struggles with and is overcome by the dominant triune soul force of the brain and body. In reality, the faulty and inferior knowledge of humans is the limited rational cerebral cortex of the brain that consists of a lesser number of total brain neurons evolved and utilized for reasoning.

The latest neuroscience research estimates that the human brain consists of some eighty-six billion neurons comprising specialized areas of function. The cerebral cortex is the predominant reasoning area of the brain and consists of sixteen billion neurons. The cerebellum regulates body posture and movement, and consists of sixty-nine billion neurons. The midbrain consist of roughly one billion neurons and regulates the subconscious autonomic, sympathetic and parasympathetic nervous system of the body. The total for non-cerebral cortex and non-reasoning neurons of the brain, consists of approximately seventy billion.

Out of a total eighty-six billion brain neurons, a minority sixteen billion or nineteen percent are possibly utilized for reasoning. The majority seventy billion or eighty-one percent non-reasoning neurons regulate the one hundred trillion cells of the body.

Four times more brain neurons are non-reasoning and regulate autonomic body functions. The majority non-reasoning neurons of the brain and body, direct the functions of cells and organs of life. Conscious reasoning only guides behaviors to acquire what the subconscious brain and body requires. Innate in the body and autonomic nervous system, cerebellum and midbrain, the subconscious triune soul force of hunger for food, sex and reproduction, and aggression, easily overwhelms conscious reasoning of the cerebral cortex.

Neuroscience further estimates that of the roughly sixteen billion neurons of the cerebral cortex, only a limited one to ten percent of them are consciously aware at any waking moment. The ability to consciously reason and to be aware during any particular moment is limited. The limitation of self and soul knowledge is the real meaning and import of the poignant lament portrayed as punishment meted out by the first father god to his created naïve humans in the Garden of Eden story.

Guilt

The Garden of Eden story conveys the message that, when created, humans were endowed with basic knowledge, acquired more knowledge, and then acquired guilt relative to a human-like god. Contrary to story, a human-like god did not impose the human sense of guilt, it was the slow evolving knowledge of how life is from which guilt originated. Humans should rightly feel guilty about a life of killing for food, sex and the reproduction of life to continue its interminable struggle and aggression. How much aggression by murder and war has been, is, and is yet to come?

Biological life is an evolving, unstable, and frequently faulty cellular construction of cells, organs, and body. Human conscious thoughts and reasoning are usually superficial, while subconscious autonomic functions of the body are primary and dominant. Life is a series of illnesses, accidents, toil and turmoil of mistakes that usually cannot be undone, and violence. How can humans sanely be proud and guilt free of their conduct in living?

Humans should feel guilty about an egocentric life of self-seeking for attention, pleasure, possessions, and opposition and aggression directed to others.

The earth is a zone of conflict, where human life conflicts with the environment, with other species, and with other individuals. Each moment on the stage of life, humans diverge in thoughts, emotions, and behaviors that cause interpersonal conflict and guilt of broken relationships, crime, and wars. The better or higher knowledge of conscience experiences guilt, and justly so.

Wise and Unwise

Humans have a difficult time comprehending cause and effect. Some cultures are much more adept at observing a real sequence of change. The wise Hindus developed the view of karma, the unerring function of cause and effect change. Greek wisdom developed observation and speculation of the origin of life from the environment, philosophy, medicine, drama of humans and gods, and sport competition of the Olympics. Some wise Chinese follow the Tao, the "way." Since the earth is a direct continuation of where all came from, the Tao, the Chinese wisely observe and follow the way of the environment. The Chinese accomplished this superb feat without the need for the model of a human-like god.

In the Middle East, the lack of intelligent observation and comprehension of the cause and effect change of environment, was compensated for by the unwise imagining of an intelligent human-like first father god. The unwise Jews proposed that an unknown and imagined first father brought them into life existence. Yet a family drama led to the first humans being cursed and condemned by the forefather god.

In every clime and time, humans are followers. They ever seek for direction to either the good or the bad, and though willful and stubborn, usually look to a leader. Dependent and vulnerable to events and situations, humans continually seek which way to go on the journey through an unrelenting sequence of life experiences.

Often lacking reliable leadership among family, friends, and politicians, humans are prone to imagine a greater human-like leader, a first father god. Who better to look to for wise leadership than an imaginary human-like god who led the biblical first humans into the tragicomedy of life?

In vivid contrast, some nontheistic ascetics comprehend they must not look to an imagined human-like god but instead observe what leads them through real life experience. Ascetics may realize they cannot rely on or follow an imagined leader. Some individuals drawn to mild or moderate asceticism intuitively sense the truth of the triune soul force. They wisely seek to discipline, fashion, and guide the immanent and destruction-resistant soul, sensed to be a continuation of a cosmological force. Not an unreal imaginary human-like god but a real triune soul force is truly worthy of comprehension, awe, respect, and reverence.

As the popular saying states, "Art imitates life." Yet art also diverts attention from life to a static painting, sculpture, or written work. An artistically imagined and word built mental sculpture of a human-like god, also diverts attention from life. During life, like weeds, thousands of wants spring up, stimulating to action and often disorientation, mishap, accident, and trauma. The ascetic withdraws from profane life, to lessen struggle with society, and to instead struggle with the triune soul force of hunger for food, sex and reproduction, and aggression. While less than a completely comfortable process, the ascetic derives joy from self and soul observation, discovery, and developing higher knowledge and wisdom based on his own efforts to comprehend.

In prejudiced theistic thinking, an imaginary human-like god is overvalued while the real soul is undervalued. The cosmos is real as is evident. The soul is real though not as perceptually evident. A human-like god is purely imaginary. A human-like god is imagined to control the environment and to intervene in human events, and to protect humans both from the environment, and from other living forms, especially other humans.

There is struggle of the conscious cerebral brain with the subconscious cerebellum and midbrain brain areas and the body. Each individual conscious self struggles with their own subconscious triune soul force of hunger for food, sex and reproduction, and aggression. The individual also struggles with the conscious self and subconscious soul force of others, including family members, friends, coworkers, fellow humans, animal, plant, and microscopic infectious life forms. An individual struggles with the non-conscious environment. All of life is permeated with effort and struggle. Individual effort and struggle is dependent on and supported by the environment, of which all is a continuation.

The triune soul force as the will to live of hunger, sex, and aggression, seldom gives up on the struggle to continue to exist in life, and will continue to exert effort to exist after death. Both the secondary conscious self, and primary subconscious soul of life, occur as a continuation of a cosmological force. In reality, a human-like god does not exist but a cosmological force does. As a continuation of a cosmological force, a human soul is at least resistant to destruction. If not able to be destroyed, the soul can at least be calmed and disciplined through asceticism to not continue to exist on earth or elsewhere.

Biological life is destructible but the soul force is at least resistant to destruction, and may not be destructible. The evidence to support this assertion, consists of reliable reported case studies of near-death experiences, verified accounts of childhood reincarnation, verified sessions of authentic mediumship, and many anecdotal after-death visits of deceased persons to family members and friends

Plato's Soul

The Greek philosopher Plato (circa 424–347 BCE) conceived of the psyche or soul as having three parts or functions. He also thought the three parts of the soul had a correspondence with three class levels of society and their own relevant virtues.

Soul	**Society**	**Virtue**
Reason	Philosophers	Wisdom
Spirited	Military	Bravery
Appetitive	Workers	Temperate

For Plato the most important and main function of the soul is reason (Greek logos), the ability to think, learn, acquire knowledge and wisdom, and to love goodness. This capability belongs to the philosophers who Plato thought are best suited to rule society. Plato also thought reason to be the most important function of the soul, and that the ability is difficult to find in the majority members of society.

Another function is the spirited, the emotional need to be approved of and accepted, anger and aggression. This part of the soul is useful in military defense and to keep civil order in society. The third function of the soul is appetitive; desires for food, drink, sex, and money.

Reason circularly conceives of the ability of the soul to reason, to which was subordinated spirited emotion and appetitive desires. Plato was mistaken in his conception of the primary function of the soul to be reason. Plato also taught that the soul survived physical death and returned to live again in a cycle of metempsychosis or reincarnation. The nonphysical soul could be polluted by an excess of spirited emotions and appetitive desires that cloud reason, so that at the time of death and separation from the body, it is drawn again to an earthly life.

For Plato, artistic images are imaginative representations of fleeting relative objects that are mere copies of a real eidos or idea, intuited only by contemplation. There is a pattern of all relative things as a class. An eidos is a mental collating of particulars into a universal template or class. Plato classified the many parts of various classes into one unified pattern or eidos.

Imagining does distract from what is real, yet so does reasoning to form one greater class of many particulars, the purpose of which is to practice the intuitive act of transcendent contemplation.

Rather than sensory distraction by particulars, by classifying them there is a unifying abstract idea. The holding of conscious attention and contemplating an eidos, such as beauty, justice, or numbers, was accepted as a way of temporarily transcending the subconscious body

Plato was correct about a tripartite psyche or soul but mistaken in his conception of it. In reality, the human soul consists of a primary triune immanent nonreasoning force of hunger for food, sex and reproduction, and aggression. The soul evolved the body over millions of years, while conscious reasoning is a secondary ability for measuring and calculation that only evolved slowly over thousands of years.

Neuroscience research does not support Plato's view that reason is the predominant function of the body. Out of a total eighty-six billion brain neurons, a minority nineteen percent or sixteen billion are possibly utilized for reasoning. The majority eighty-one percent or seventy billion neurons regulate the one hundred trillion cells of the body. The cerebral cortex of the human brain consists of sixteen billion neurons of which neuroscience estimates that only from one percent to ten percent (one hundred million to one billion six hundred thousand) are consciously aware at any particular waking moment. The ability to be aware and to reason in any given moment is limited.

Speculating, at the time of death the soul may separate from the physical body, to super-position and exist inter-dimensionally. Further speculating, the triune soul may be only from one to ten percent conscious, and the remaining ninety-nine to ninety percent subconscious, with a mere nineteen percent capability for reasoning.

Soul and Self

The word soul is derived from Old English, sawol, Old Norse, sala, Old High German, seula.

The soul is said to be an animating spiritual part of a person. The word spirit is from Latin spiritus, meaning breath, and spirare, to breathe. The soul has little to do with the spirit or breathing of a person. Soul is the vital force of life, and is what subconsciously moves cells and organs to function.

Only during the twentieth century did the field of psychology became a recognized profession. During this time, psychologists began to prefer not to use the word soul to refer to a human being. The term soul is of course associated with religion, so the field of psychology began to use and popularize the word, self. The word self, is from Old English selfa or seolf. In modern parlance, the term self has replaced use of the word soul. The word self is defined as, "conscious willing and knowing, identity, character, and personality traits."

As a continuation of a sole cosmological force, the triune soul force constructs and organizes both the subconscious functions and the conscious human self. To contrast, the word self refers to conscious willing, knowing, and personality traits. It is the soul that actively constructs life, repairs cellular injuries, replicates and reproduces, survives death, and may even live again.

Human-like God

Theistic religions present with a collective variant of a gender identity disorder (GID), the severe symptom of which is the aberrant attribution of a human-like male god to be the origin of existence. Instead of a large number of individuals being confused about their own gender identity, many are confused about where life came from, confused about the toil and turmoil of living, and what will happen after physical death. The simplistic solution for many years, has been to imagine a supernatural numerical first father that is the origin of all genealogical natural fathers, and mothers. To comprehend the order and disorder of life, as many young children do, adults similarly imagine a companion, assign a gender of a first father, and project it onto the ungendered origin of the environment and life.

Out of desperation and limited knowledge of how to relieve existential angst, and seeking protection from disaster, destruction, and death, a great many susceptible humans accept a parental gender as a way to make known an unknown beginning of their woes of living. For those who have in childhood acquired the theistic gender identity disorder from adults, the prognosis for such afflicted individuals is but a poor to moderate chance for a full therapeutic recovery.

A human-like god is offered by religious authorities who stimulate and entice the psychological imagination of the gullible. Theistic religion deceptively offers to the desperate, a devised imaginary helper for the helpless. A human-like god is a human way of finding imagined favor in the unfavorable conditions of life, and to obtain a particular advantage. To accept there is a human-like god, humans can then receive the certainty of good intentions from the deity rather than rely on uncertain environmental cause and effect change. A human-like god is a way humans uplift themselves with the hope and expectation that the difficulties of life will be favorably resolved in their favor.

Humans give mealtime thanks to a human-like god for available food to consume. Humans give thanks to the god for the sexual conception of children. Thanks is given for assistance and protection prior to aggression in any hazardous behavior, such as during times of war. Though humans continue to be unsafe during life on earth, when death ensues, a safe afterlife haven is said to be provided and administered by the god. Vulnerable humans provide themselves with the courage for life by artistically fashioning and utilizing a human-like god.

Humans have propped themselves up through use of a prop in the theatrical drama of life. The word prop as a noun is defined as, "a pole or beam used as support to keep something in position, an object not an integral part of the thing supported; a portable object used on the set of a play or movie." The prop of a human-like god is used to support humans, to keep them in a tolerable position of life. A god has been placed above and beyond humans to serve as a foundation of support beneath them.

A humanlike god is imagined and used as a prop in the theatrical play, the movie drama and comedy of life. A human-like god is a prop, a supportive way humans comprehend what has propelled the environment and life into existence.

Like the real sun, the conceived and imaginary human-like god, brightens up an otherwise dark and dismal earthly life of individual toil, turmoil, and troubles. A god is a way of imagining goodness on an earth that is at least fifty percent not good. Human imagination surrounds life on earth with good and surrounds an afterlife with half goodness and half evil of heaven and hell. Humans then have the burden of choosing what is good over evil.

One of the mottos of the United States as found on its currency is, "In god we trust." Humans should have trust in a shared metaphysical cosmic force that moves all things. Existence must be looked at as not coming from a human-like god that shapes all things from outside but as a subtle cosmological force surrounding and immanent within all things.

While taking an oath in a court of law to tell the truth with the phrase "…so help you god," one should refuse to respond to a false referent. This is so, as a god is a subjective mental conception of a human-like presence that does not objectively exist. Why invoke a false concept when truth is sought?

Pleasure

An individual goes from minute to minute thinking, "I have this pleasure, or I want that pleasure." There is always an effort to obtain or retain a pleasure. Yet much pain occurs from failure to obtain a pleasure or from loss of a pleasure.

In reality, as a continuation of the earth and a cosmological force, humans are forced by the triune soul force to obtain the pleasures of eating food, having sex and reproducing, and expressing aggression. Seeking of pleasures is the effort to avert, reduce, and to remove pain.

Eating of food is the pleasure of escaping the pain of hunger. Having sex is the pleasure of escaping the pain of frustration, and reproduction is the pleasure of having a part of one's own body to relieve loneliness and to be of help. Physical and verbal aggression is the pleasure of reducing or removing frustration and limitations.

Pleasure prolonged becomes a pain. Pleasures are difficult to obtain, and an individual often longs to repeat them. Wanting of pleasures provides meaning, and when desire wanes, there is a loss of meaning for the object and wanting to have it.

A human-like god is the imaginary way to obtain and to continue to experience pleasures rather than pains. A god also represents the strength to persevere and to endure through pain experiences. A god can be appealed to for strength to have the pleasure of inflicting pain and revenge on others, and for the pleasure of dominance and control. A god is the pleasurable imaginary thought of having protection and provides the courage to endure and to continue to live and to die. The willing of an imaginary human-like god supplements human willing of life, and is a way of obtaining pleasure in an afterlife.

What is good is a pleasure. A god is the imaginary bringer of good that is of course pleasurable. Yet, a good god is merely human imagining and seeking of alleviation of pain and suffering, and is a way of obtaining a greater and longer lasting pleasure. For some, merely thinking of the idea of a human-like god is pleasurable. A god is the pleasure of transcending ignorance and of knowing the beginning, overcoming fear, and having protection in life and death.

Many humans say they come from a human-like god, must be godlike and good in behavior, and will bask in the presence of a human-like god after death. Seeking the pleasure of safety in both life and death, humans use words to artistically smear their own likeness into a mental model of a human-like god. An imaginary human-like god is emphasized to be beyond the earth, and if favored by offerings or good ethical conduct, the god will then help humans.

Nephesh

The Jews have long lacked the concept of a soul and instead used the word nephesh, translated into English as soul. Genesis 2:7 states, "And the Lord God formed man of the dust of the ground, and breathed into his nostrils the breath of life; and man became a living soul." The phrase translated as, living soul, is the Hebrew word nephesh, meaning, animated and alive.

The Hebrew word nephesh, means, "the essence of life, the act of breathing, taking a breath." (Vine's Complete Expository Dictionary of Old and New Testament Words) Further, use of the word nephesh in the Old Testament, "…never means the immortal soul, but it is essentially the life principle, or the living being…." (The Interpreter's Dictionary of the Bible) To destroy the nephesh, is to destroy an individual's ability to breathe, and body to live. Use of the word nephesh first occurs in Genesis 1:21. According to this usage, animals were animated and alive, as are humans. The second use of the word is Genesis 1:24.

"And God created great whales, and every living creature [nephesh] that moveth, which the waters brought forth abundantly, after their kind, and every winged fowl after his kind: and God saw that it was good." (Genesis 1:21)

"And God said, Let the earth bring forth the living creature [nephesh] after his kind, cattle, and creeping thing, and beast of the earth after his kind: and it was so." (Genesis 1:24)

In Genesis 2:19, animals are also referred to as having or being nephesh. "Whatsoever Adam called every living creature [nephesh] that was the name thereof." Genesis 9:4-5 states that what animates life is not a soul but the blood.

"But flesh with the life [nephesh] thereof, which is the blood thereof, shall ye not eat.

And surely your blood of your lives [nephesh] will I require; at the hand of every beast will I require it, and at the hand of man; at the hand of every man's brother will I require the life [nephesh] of man."

Both humans and animals have a life consisting of breath and blood, and after death all go to the same place, the soil of the earth. Theists tend to think of themselves as better than animals. Yet according to the book of Ecclesiastes written circa 200 BCE, this view is not correct.

"For that which befalleth the sons of men befalleth beasts; even one thing befalleth them: as the one dieth, so dieth the other; yea, they have all one breath [ruah] so that a man hath no preeminence above a beast: for all is vanity. All go unto one place; all are of the dust, and all to dust return again." (Ecclesiastes 3:19-20)

Yet humans have it better than animals as at least they have a chance for their body to be resurrected by a human-like god on the Day of Judgement.

Destruction Resistant Soul

In the biblical Genesis story, the human-like god who made a miraculous creation did not remedy the good and evil knowledge obtained by the first two humans. The god's response was to punish the first humans by cursing them. Later, the ingested good and evil fruit was not expunged by the god from the two humans. The evil not able to be removed is in reality, the triune soul force of hunger for food, sex and reproduction, and aggression. An imaginary human-like god cannot remove from a person of what in reality is an innate real soul as the continuation of the environment and a cosmological force.

I define evil as excessive force, especially of aggression and harm directed by one human toward another. The problem of evil aggression cannot be removed from life, nor can hunger, and sex and reproduction be removed as they are the triune soul essence of life. Evil can be modified and reduced but never expunged.

In the religion of Judaism, the place where evil humans go to be punished is Gehenna, originally the dump where garbage was burned outside of Jerusalem. The individual will dwell in the fire of Gehenna for no longer than twelve months. Afterwards, the individual may proceed to a heaven. Some individuals, such as seducers and blasphemers, remain in Gehenna and undergo eternal tortures without ceasing. (Jewish Encyclopedia)

In Christianity, evil individuals will be tortured for an eternity by burning in the fires of Hell, meaning Gehenna. In the religion of Islam evil persons will be tortured by fire for an eternity or until Allah stops the process. The god of these theistic religions does not destroy human souls, he only tortures them as punishment. This scenario testifies to the indestructability of the soul. In reality, the real willful human triune soul is greater than an imaginary willful human-like god.

Westernized Christianity says that a human soul is made by a human-like god. In reality, a soul is a continuation of a cosmological force, and therefore must be resistant to being destroyed or oblivion. That this is recognized by humans on some level of awareness, is that in any theistic god story there is no mention of the actual act of destroying a human soul. An omnipotent god is imaginary and therefore cannot destroy a real human soul. In imaginary story, a human-like god can only inflict suffering and torture on an evil individual. The theistic statements of punishment of the soul are many mentioned in Zoroastrianism texts, Old and New Testaments, and the Quran.

Zoroastrian writings say that at the end of a three thousand year cycle, the good human-like spirit or god Ahura Mazada will destroy the evil of existence, and there will be a judgment day. The god will resurrect the dead and judge them. The good will be rewarded with a resurrected physical body or an eternal life in a heaven, and the evil will variously be purified and resurrected, spend either a limit of nine thousand years, or eternal suffering in a dark and fiery foul smelling place (Drugodemana, house of wrong or destruction) under the earth.

The religion of Islam states that whoever practices another religion and who does not accept and submit to the human-like god Allah, will after death, exist without help and will undergo painful punishment.

"Whoever seeks a religion other than Islam, it will not be accepted from him, and he will be a loser in the hereafter." (Quran 3:85) "Those who have not believed and died, the earth full of gold and offered as ransom would not be accepted. They will have a painful punishment and they will have no help. (Quran 3:91)

In Christian writings, Jesus is portrayed as speaking the words of a verse in Luke, stating that a human-like god, after killing a person, has the power to cast a deceased individual into a burning Hell or Gehenna.

"And I say unto you my friends. Be not afraid of them that kill the body, and after that have no more that they can do. But I will forewarn you whom you shall fear: Fear him, which after he hath killed hath power to cast into hell [Gehenna]; yea, I say unto you, Fear him." (Luke 12:5-6)

The verse states that the god kills (Greek thuo) the physical body but there is no mention of a soul. There is a general warning of what appears to be the potential destruction of a human soul. Yet the verse is a poor translation and therefore deceptive in meaning.

"And fear not them which kill the body, but are not able to kill the soul [nephesh]: but rather fear him which is able to destroy both soul and body in hell [Gehenna]." (Matthew 10:28)

In the Matthew verse the god will not kill but will destroy (Greek apollumi) both the body and the life (Hebrew nephesh, Greek psuche) of the body. Jesus advises to not be afraid of those who can kill the body as they cannot kill the life, translated as soul.

The remainder of the verse says an individual should be afraid of a human-like god who is able to destroy both the life and the body in Gehenna, the large burning garbage dump located outside of Jerusalem.

Depending on context, the Greek word, apollumi, has various meanings. The New Testament uses the word at least ninety times to variously mean, perish thirty-three times, lost or to lose, thirty-one times, and destroy, twenty-six times.

Jesus does not say the god will kill the life and the body but that the god will destroy (Greek apollumi) the body and therefore the ability to live by burning it to ashes in the garbage fire of Gehenna. In other words, he will discard and burn all human trash. There are other mentions by Jesus of fire and the burning of individuals after death.

"If a man abide not in me, he is cast forth as a branch, and is withered; and men gather them, and cast them into the fire, and they are burned." (John 15:6) "Let both grow together until the harvest: and in the time of harvest I will say to the reapers, Gather ye together first the tares, and bind them in bundles to burn them: but gather the wheat into my barn." (Matthew 13: 30)

Dry branches are gathered for firewood. The tares or bad weeds coexist with the good wheat plants, and at harvest time the two are separated. The wheat is saved in the barn while the weeds are discarded and burnt. Those humans who are like weeds and serve no useful purpose will be burned and destroyed.

There is no soul in Jewish or Israelite thinking, only the nephesh or life. Christian English speaking Catholic and Protestant religions translate nephesh as soul, and therefore have imposed the meaning that there is an immortal presence in the body that differs from and animates it. So there is a mix of meaning in the words attributed to Jesus. His words meant one thing to him and his hearers, and another meaning to later Christians.

What Jesus may have meant by the life (nephesh) being discarded into the flames of Gehenna, is that the ability to live will be destroyed as the god will refuse to resurrect them. Jesus may also have meant that the quality of life and individual happiness or well-being will certainly perish, be lost, or be destroyed. The individual in Gehenna or Hell will burn and the quality of their life will perish, be lost, or be destroyed. The opportunity to "live" or have a life (nephesh) with the god and the good in heaven will perish, be lost, or be destroyed.

It is stated that when Jesus returns, evil will be removed from the earth by separating the good from those who are evil. (John 5:28-29; Matthew 13:40-43) Why wait for the world to come of the Last Judgment to separate those good humans from any evil individuals? In reality, no imaginary god can separate the good from evil persons while living on earth, only a real human government can do so. Since a humanlike god is imaginary, then humans have the burden of separating themselves from the evil willing of fellow humans in life and any afterlife.

Later Christian writings speak of a hell (Anglo Saxon, helan, hole, cave, and hiding place) as a lake of fire which the god has created to inflict suffering on an individual but will not destroy the life or soul. Hell is a place for the damned, those separated from the god and those who are good. John the disciple, said to be the author of the *Book of Revelation,* relates how a voice from heaven declared to him the following:

"I will give unto him that is athirst of the fountain of the water of life freely...But the fearful, and unbelieving, and the abominable, and murders, and whoremongers, and sorcerers, and idolaters, and all liars, shall have their part in the lake which burneth with fire and brimstone: which is the second death. (Revelation 21:6, 8)

The preponderance of the evidence is both convincing and is beyond a reasonable doubt.

As the words of Jesus suggest, the biblical god is a killer of the human biological body, (Genesis chapters 6-9) and a destroyer of the nephesh or life by the god not resurrecting evil individuals, and perhaps a destroyer of the quality of human life. For later Christians, the god is not a destroyer of souls but a punisher and torturer of them.

Looking over the recorded events in the life struggles of Jesus as portrayed in the gospels, the overall message of the Christian religion can be stated in this way. From a bloody menstruating womb has come each human life, a life in which an individual's blood is shed either suddenly through accident or violence, or slowly through a lifetime of ageing to finally reach an end in death. From being born in blood, and shedding the blood of physical wounds and many emotional hurts during a lifetime, a nonblood triune soul that forces the body to live, departs and enters a bloodless afterlife dimension.

Soul Force

As the human body wears and ages, and ability and agility fade, a large percentage of the population think that some greater human-like god who made them will also save them. Only in the previous seventy-five years or so, has a small number of individuals been able to see life as an evolving and dependent continuation of the environment.

The challenge for the twenty-first century is to be able to perceive both life and the environment, to be a continuation of a cosmological force. Humans vaguely sense that they are a continuation of some kind of transcendent origin beyond the visible environment, and this basic intuition is correct. Yet, it is an error to conceive of the transcendent origin of life and humans to be a human-like god. The true transcendental origin is a cosmological force, and the continuation of it is a triune soul force as the will to live of hunger, sex, and aggression.

As a continuation of a cosmological force, the triune soul force of hunger for food, sex and reproduction, and aggression, may not wear out. Instead it seems, the triune soul wears out the biological cells and organs of the living body. As the cells, organs, muscles, bones, and hormones of the body age, the driving force of hunger, sex, and aggression become less and less until physical death. Biological parts can only function for a limited time but as a continuation of a cosmological force, the triune soul cannot wear out. As a continuation of a cosmological force, the animating immanence of a triune soul may transcend the death of the human body.

The essence from which energy, environmental forms, and life has come, is not a human-like god but a pure cosmological force. Humans recognize that the environment and life is in motion, and that life moves and changes dependent on a changing environment. Humans have primitively identified the impetus for related now motion as a human-like first father god. In reality, all relative motion is a continuation of a cosmological force.

A local force such as strong or weak nuclear force may change and dissipate. So may the local force of magnetism of a natural magnet, and the gravity force of a mass in space will change and dissipate in time. The local phenomena of mass, energy, and force may dissipate. In so doing, a phenomenon reverts (Latin re, again, and, vertere, to turn) to where it came from, it goes back or returns to a previous or former condition. As a continuation of a nonlocal cosmological force, all local forces, energy, and mass, revert to its dimension of origin.

From a cosmological force comes changing verb energy and noun elements and forms of the environment. On earth evolved life forms moved by a subconscious triune soul force of hunger for food, sex and reproduction, and aggression. As a noun and changing verb part and continuation of the environment, harmony among parts of the human body and brain/mind functions is difficult to maintain. Paradise has never existed for any living form.

Humans are either searching for food, eating, avoiding or escaping being eaten; a person is either searching for sex, having sex, avoiding or escaping the results of it; and an individual is either avoiding, escaping, or inflicting aggression.

Human life evolves to live and to know more about a life that consists of willful struggle and of making and unmaking problems. Life is a maze of sensations, thoughts, memories, imaginations, and behaviors, one's own and others, trial and error learning, true and false knowledge, distractions, fears, and confusions. Through accidents, illnesses, mistakes; the brief pleasures and long pains of toil and obtaining food, sex and caring for the results of reproduction, and one's own or others aggressions; each individual endures a brief life. Each person is a performer on the stage of reality as a continuation of an ever-forming cosmological force.

Individual human life is far from ideal, rulers and governments are not ideal, and the environment is acceptable but less than ideal. Humans have the ability to idealize. Tracing life to the distant and unknown past, humans idealized the beginning of the genealogical line of fathers by conceiving of a caring human-like first father god.

Soul Dynamic

The triune soul force consists of both a primary subconscious and secondary conscious pulling, pushing, and straining in the body and brain. Efforts are directed to obtain food, obtain sex and reproduce and care for children, and a subconscious and conscious straining in the body and brain for aggression. This pulling, pushing and straining occurring in body and brain is popularly referred to as the "will to live." This is a synonym for the word soul, popularly said to exist in the biological body and to survive physical death.

Material forms consist of atoms and electrons, and there is a lack of internal pulling and straining to survive and exist as there is in living forms. It is the animating pulling, pushing, and straining that forms a pattern in the energy of elements of which the body and brain consists, and also in the energy field of elements of the earth environment.

Life exists not only as a form, the energy of life also forms a pattern in a surround of a cosmological force, field, or ground.

The human body and brain are composed of a genetically determined pattern of molecules that are a continuation of and are determined by elements of energy consisting of atoms and electrons. The empirically verified scientific second theorem of thermodynamics, known as, the conservation of energy, states that "the total energy of a closed system cannot be created or destroyed but changes and is conserved over time." Since energy of material forms is conserved and transformed, then so is the energy of living forms conserved and transformed. Unlike living forms, material forms lack a will to live of a triune soul and therefore lack a cluster pattern of force that is resistant to destruction.

The subconscious and conscious patterns of pulling, pushing, and straining of the will to live occur in a physical body and brain composed of organic molecules and elements of energy as atoms and electrons. Life occurs as a dependent continuation of the atom and electron energy field of the earth. The earth and galactic environment occurs as a continuation of relative forces of gravity and electromagnetism, and these are nestled in and are a continuation of a cosmological force, field, or ground.

The molecular and biological form of life is brief but not the essence of what moves it. The body is a continuation of relative energy while the soul is a relative pattern of force that exists as a continuation of cosmological force. This being so, the soul can continue to exist as a coherent pattern amid the dimensional properties of space-time.

The triune soul consisting of the force of hunger for food, sex and reproduction, and aggression, is a continuation of a cosmological force, and as such is at least resistant to if not immune to destruction. The true problem of existence is to reduce and resolve the conscious and subconscious individual pattern of willing, and to guide it to quiescence.

No imagined human-like god can grant peace to a human soul in life or an afterlife. Each individual brings peace to his own existence.

Ancestor

Many find comfort even in the capitalized word of a greater universal God. Making use of the imaginary companion of a human-like god, humans seek to accept and to include others. Theists promote the view that there is a human-like god who is the ancestor and first father of all humans. The conceived model of a human-like god serves as a shared father figure. It is hoped by theists that by having a shared first father, humans will see themselves as members of the same family.

Using the metaphor of a human-like first father god, it is hoped that humans will be able to get along, and be accepting, kind, helpful, loving, forgiving, and not harm a fellow family member. Having a human-like first father god who loves his humans, (except for those he will punish in an afterlife), humans can identify with this attitude and imitate it in their thoughts, emotions, and behaviors toward each other. However, an imaginary ego cannot possibly solve the problems of real egocentric humans.

Despite an imagined comforting fatherly god model, it is a long term reality that members of even a small nuclear family have much difficulty getting along. There exists family violence, spouse abuse, child abuse, runaway children, rape, crime, and murder of family members. These behaviors are all too prevalent, have always existed, and will unfortunately continue unabated into the future.

Theists seek to join humans into one big happy family by having a human-like first father god. Yet, by subjectively knowing the origin of existence to be a supernatural ancestor and genealogical first father god, theists perforce separate themselves from a shared environmental origin. There is a super nature but it is not a human-like god, it is a cosmological force shared by all of life as a triune soul that forces life to live.

Humans egocentrically separate from each other by not seeing a shared biology and a triune soul force, and instead see differences of appearance, ideas, values, and behaviors. To truly see into the depth of a person, is to focus on and ponder their attitude toward food, sex and reproduction, and how they handle or express aggression. This is the essence of what a person truly is, aside from plain likes and dislikes.

The common way of viewing an ancestor is that this person is from whom I have descended, whose name is such and such, to whom I bear a physical resemblance, and who lived to a certain age. This is the accepted and common way a person sees his forebears. A more objective way of seeing one's ancestors is for the person to see themselves as descended from and as a continuation of a triune soul force of hunger for food, sex and the reproductive act, and adequate aggression to have survived. Each is the sexual product of parents, and they of parents the same are the product of their hunger and obtaining of food and of aggressively competing to survive.

This is the true usually unnoticed reality, and there is a need to develop a practice of seeing reality as it really is. The triune soul of an individual and that of his ancestors, is a continuation of a sole cosmological force.

Value and Devalue

It is a matter of debate as to what percentage of life is bad, evil, or suffering. Is it fifty percent, twenty-five, ten or even one percent? Whatever percentage appeals to an individual estimate, early humans had to have pondered the value of life.

In those cultures that subjectively imagined and developed a traditional acceptance of a human-like god, it was thought that surely the origin of life must value life. If humans do not value life, then surely a human-like first father god of life does so. Yet no human-like god has ever convincingly intervened in human affairs to improve the value of life except by way of selective and subjective interpretation.

Among members of any human group, individuals devalue each other daily through a creative series of abrasive differences and minor irritations. If increased, these daily irritations frequently lead to serious conscious and subconscious conflict and behavioral aggression. This is the norm and is popularly said to be, "Getting on someone's nerves."

Humans usually undervalue each other on a personal level, and countries fail to value other groups and cultures. Therefore a human-like god is conceived to exist, as a human way of vicariously valuing life as does the imagined maker of it. To learn to live without an imaginary human-like god is not easy. This is so as a god is conflated with an afterlife dimension. Not having a god is equated with not having an afterlife dimension, and therefore no individual survival. While personal oblivion is an acceptable alternative for the many disappointments and sorrows of life, few can tolerate the thought of it.

Letting go of the view of a human-like god is synonymous with letting go of surviving life and entry into an afterlife. Something or someone has to be in charge of life and the afterlife dimension. Humans realize it is difficult to save themselves as they are slow to learn and focus mainly on the mundane details and differences of everyday life. Lazy humans have little interest in investigation and learning; most only follow an unthinking theistic religious tradition and rely on blind faith in an imagined human-like god.

Despite the encouragement of theistic religions, good deeds while beneficial, cannot serve to save an individual. Good deeds are their own reward. Only knowledge and wisdom can save an individual. Good deeds said to please a human-like god, in reality only please and comfort other humans and the egocentric individual.

Humans are always interested in doing good to please themselves and slightly interested in pleasing other frail humans. However, many are most interested in doing good to please a human-like god, a god powerful enough to reward or punish them.

While the concept of a god may encourage good deeds to be done to avoid punishment, focus on a god may also lead to a disregard for good toward fellow humans. Instead of pleasing fellow humans, a theist may terrorize and kill them to please an imagined god.

Roots of Life

The primitive notion of a human-like god parroted by so many, is an embarrassment to the clarity of comprehension. A human-like god can be seen to be an immature, foreign, and false insertion into a real dynamic sequence of cause and effect change. The roots of life extend into the cells and organs of the body, and retracing the origin of the parts extends to the environment, and further extend to a cosmological force. The force that moves the living parts of the body is a triune soul force, and its dynamic roots grow from the earth and from the rootless ground of a cosmological force.

The roots of life can be traced to its origin. Life consists of organs and these consists of cells that consists of functioning parts. The functioning parts of cells are a dependent continuation of the environment, the elements of earth, water, air, temperature, and photons of light. The parts of the environment are a dependent continuation of relative energy elements, weak and strong nuclear forces, magnetism, and gravity. These are a continuation of a cosmological force.

The parts of living cells move and are moved by a dynamic force known as the will to live. The will to live is the triune soul force of hunger for food, sex and reproduction, and aggression that is a continuation of a sole cosmological force.

When living cells are damaged, the elements of energy that make up life are not destroyed. According to the empirically verified scientific theorem of thermodynamics known as, the conservation of energy, the total energy of a closed system cannot be created or destroyed but changes and is only conserved over time. Life is nestled in the nursery of the environment that is a continuation of energy and a cosmological force.

As a relative soul force is a continuation of a sole cosmological force, it is relatively destructible and is conserved through time changes.

It is only the environment, the social milieu, and personal intelligence that supports and convincingly instructs each individual what to do, rather than does an imagined human-like first father god. The environment and life does not come from any kind of intelligence or reasoning. Only from impaired and simplistic human reasoning of the brain has come a conceived human-like reasonable god.

A conceived human-like god is a cognitive tool, an artifact utilized to overcome the unreasoning triune soul force of hunger for food, sex and reproduction, and aggression. The model of a human-like god is artistically erected as a vicarious way of obtaining safety in an often unknown sequence of unsafe reality experience prone to mishaps and serious mistakes that result in illness, injury, and death.

A god is the result of human effort to rationalize the beginning of human existence, and to make rational sense of an irrational life and death experience. A human-like god is the fervent and often futile effort to influence humans to be rational. The metaphor of a loving first father god serves as a model for unloving and barbaric earthly fathers. A human-like god is a psychological reaction formation to the unreasoning and irrational function of the brain and body, and a non-reasoning environment.

Humans find it difficult to comprehend a cause and effect reality of change. Having a vicarious relationship with an imaginary numerical first father god who better comprehends existence, can substitute for the often feeble human comprehension of reality.

Higher Knowledge

The imagining and conceptual artistic crafting of a human-like first father god is a human reflex response, both to the evils of the environment and the aggression inside other life forms, especially in humans. Individuals know they are dependent and vulnerable. What the group to which one belongs, thinks and does, is important for survival.

Therefore, it is important to know how to interact with the greater number of other humans. Having the innate and evolved ability for memory and conscience, this human faculty is also projected outward and humanized to be a human-like god. Human conscience (of feeling good or bad about thoughts or deeds done or undone) is crafted to be a human-like god who can reward or punish. The innate ability to feel good, or to feel guilt and regret, is projected outward to be an observing and judgmental human-like god.

A conceived human-like god is a way of denoting where the environment and life came from. The contrived concept of a god, is a stamping of human likeness on the beginning of the environment and life. The notion of a god is a limited human way of reasoning and thinking about the origin of the environment and life. A god is just a way of exalting human reason and of where it came from, an idealized intelligent reasoning first father. In the Jewish story of Genesis, life came into existence from the knowing and words of a first father god. Only later did human life come from the sexual reproduction and evolution of many generations.

The god designed and endowed humans with genitals, so why is it any great surprise in the Garden of Eden that they explored and acquired some of the god's own knowledge of how to use them? The god chose not to remove the knowledge of nudity and sex and reproduction from the first humans, instead he chose to curse them. Therefore, each person today is on their own handling their hunger for food, sex and reproduction, and aggression.

Through story, humans have placed their own words in the mouths of gods to speak.

It is a human judgment when the human-like god of Genesis condemns and curses the first humans and the generations that follow through time. Human conscious reasoning is projected onto the god, as it condemns and curses the unreasoning soul force felt as hunger for food, sex and reproduction, and aggression, inside of humans. Human reason exalts its status by imagining and relating with the greater reasoning of a human-like first father god who knows all, and through use of thoughts and words of reason makes the environment and life. Human reason glorifies its origin by imagining it has come from reason.

In reality, the conscious reasoning human self has evolved from an unreasoning subconscious soul of hunger for food, sex and reproduction, and aggression. The unreasoning soul of life is a continuation of an unreasoning semi-orderly environment, and both are a continuation of a nonreasoning cosmological force.

Many thinkers have praised and exalted reason to be the main function of the soul. In reality, conscious reason is a lesser function that only guides the greater subconscious unreasoning soul of appetite for food, sex, and aggression. Human conscious thinking and knowing is often faulty, while the subconscious is mostly unthinking and unknowing, except for recall of dreams during sleep, and autonomic cellular and organ functions.

The preferred and supposed better knowing of conscious human reason is often ineffective, and an imaginary god does nothing. The human reasoning brain can only improve the now moments of life by hoping and looking to the future for opportunity and improvements. The conceived and imagined god can only inspire humans with the idea of a greater goodness, human cooperation, a life of more pleasure than pain, and an afterlife.

For the Jews there is an historical sin, (Hebrew hata, separation) a separation from a human-like god. In reality, the Garden of Eden story is a lament about obtaining or having lower knowledge and having a lack of higher knowledge as does the first father.

What truly separates humans is having an inadequate lower knowledge that differs from a projected higher knowledge, as a conceived and imagined human-like numerical first father god. Human feeble and faulty conscious knowing is dominated by the subconscious and strong triune soul of life. Help for this evolved life was imagined to be a god.

The lament about feeble or inadequate knowledge is echoed in other cultures as well. There is a faulty or inadequate human knowing that results in the Greek drama tragedies of fate. There is knowledge limiting maya or delusion of the senses and ideas in Hinduism, and limiting avidya or ignorance in both Hinduism and Buddhism. Both cause the limiting pains and limited pleasures of repetitive lifetimes of reincarnation.

Humans recognize a potential ability for higher learning, knowing, and doing, and also the potential and ability for lower knowing and doing. Lower human knowing is expressed by the subconscious body and soul as hunger for food, sex and reproduction, and aggression. Higher knowing consists of conscious reasoning, intuition, inspiration and invention, and waking and dream visions. The human potential and ability for higher knowing, is also conceived and imagined to be a supernatural intelligent human-like god.

Behavior of the Cosmos

A law (Old Norse lag, that which is laid down) is that which is laid down as a guide to behavior. When someone, "Lays down the law," they speak as an authority or in a dogmatic manner. So far as is known, laws exist only from a human perspective.

The phrase "law of nature" first appeared in the legal and law-loving administrative government of Roman culture. The phrase was used by the philosopher/poet Lucretius (99-55 BCE), poet Ovid (died circa 17 CE), and the poet Virgil (70 BCE-19 CE). The phrase was used by Roman Stoic philosopher and writer Seneca (4 BCE to 65 CE), and by lawyer and writer Pliny (23- 79 CE).

In Europe, philosopher, jurist, scientist, and the father of empiricism, Francis Bacon (1561-1626) and astronomer Galileo (1564-1642) both developed empirical observation and testing. During this time "laws of nature" were spoken of as a way of separating developing science from the laws and commandments of religion.

Natural law is a term referred to by philosophers Thomas Hobbes (1588-1679) and Baruch Spinoza (1632-1677). The phrase "natural law" is a philosophical and political view that advocates certain rights are inherent or innate in human nature, and are recognized as such by human reason.

A scientific law is defined as, "A theory or principle deduced from confirmed facts, applied to a defined group or class of phenomena, and expressed by a statement that a particular phenomenon always occurs if certain conditions are present." The environment is in motion and therefore has a behavior pattern. Humans have long observed this often mysterious behavior and sought to better comprehend it.

There is not so much laws of nature as there are behaviors of environment. Human behavior is a continuation of the behavior of the environment. Behavior is defined as, "The way in which something functions. The actions or reactions of an energy, material, or living form to an external or internal stimulus or environment."

A law implies a law-maker, something human-like, a god. There are no natural laws, only natural behavior patterns of environment and living forms. In brief, science studies behaviors, not laws. Physicists are actually psychologists, (Greek psyche, soul) of the environment. They look for an unseen unified sole cosmological force, and some study to comprehend the animating force and behavior of quantum energy and material forms. Some cosmologists seek to comprehend the animating origin of life.

By studying the behavior of the environment, human folklore and eventually modern science, has learned to influence and predict, not laws but the change and recurring behavior patterns of the environment.

There are no laws, only a panoply of animated orderly or disorderly behaviors that comprise a whole cosmos. Empirical and so-called laws of motion, electromagnetism, and gravity, are all behavior patterns. What has set the behavior of the cosmos in motion is a cosmological force. The notion of a human-like god and his laws are projected onto the behaviors of the environment. Yet for many, this way of thinking is a necessary aberration and delusion.

A law cannot be observed, only a pattern of behavior of an environmental or living form can be observed. A law is an abstract term for the relative order of a condition, event, or behavior. A law is composed of human observation and expectation. Nature (Latin natus, to be born) is born to function as a cause and effect sequence of disorder and order, as a pattern of behavior. Unfortunately, nature's behaviors are capped by and said to be made by and function according to the laws of a human-like god who imposed them. The brash human ego must intervene.

A law is composed of human observation and expectation. A law is a rule of conduct that applies only to human life on the earth and to no other living or environmental form. Nature is a regularity of order and disorder, a pattern of behavior, such as rain or drought. Behind phenomena and as impetus for the behavior of the environment is a cosmological force that imparts forms and patterns of behavior. The animated growing of life is of course a continuation of an animated going of elements, atoms, and electrons. Both environment and life are animated forms of a sole cosmological force. The environment and life divide from a cosmological force as an active divine (Latin di, into and vine as a verb to grow) patterns of form and behavior.

Each and every god that is said to exist is an artistic subjective construct in the human brain.

There is no human-like god that imposes natural laws of order that the environment, life, and humans obey. Only human efforts of religion and government seek to impose laws that regulate social order. While individual behavior may or may not follow human-made laws, all humans respond to and obey the behavior of the environment.

Enlightenment

Hunger for food, sex and reproduction, and aggression, are the triune soul that forces life to live. The soul is the impetus that enables life to survive. The triune soul forces an individual to act in the waking dream of living. The hunger for food forces life to obtain nourishment. The strong urge and tension for sex and to reproduce, forces life to find a partner. Aggression forces life to express it in surging emotions and behaviors. Subconsciously forced to act in these specific ways, humans are never consciously free. Conscious awareness and reason, can only attempt to adjust behavior to fit situations, with more or less success.

Enlightenment is the ability to see within, is the process of calming sensations of the senses by closing the eyes and sitting in a quiet place. Quieting attention to sensations, attention can then be focused to observe the brain making of space-time picture images of now, past, and future. Meditatively observing this hypnotic flow of images, the individual either soon falls asleep or manages to calm the process. No longer observing a flow of picture images, attention may then come to observe the soul that forces life to exist and to behave. Bliss comes from reducing the strong driving soul force of life.

Enlightenment is to see that a human-like god is an imaginary companion, enhanced by artistic imagining. A human-like god is the greater Go of the changing environment, and is a continuation of a cosmological force that moves all things into, through and out of existence. Enlightenment or in a theistic sense realizing god, is to have an even higher knowledge of seeing the driving soul force as cosmologically capable of after life and interdimensional existence.

This is convincingly supported by the many historical and modern anecdotal reports of near-death experience, childhood remembrances of past lives, and by convincing readings by authentic mediums.

Denouement

In the inspiring words of the Hindu saint, Ramakrishna (1836-1886): "He is born in vain who, having attained the human birth, so difficult to get, does not attempt to realize God in this very life."

To realize a human-like god is to illuminate the god-making process. To realize a god, is to know that any and all human-like gods are imaginary companions and artistic expressions of the human brain. Humans must grow up, as individuals and as a species, to realize that gods are human-like as they are always human made.

To realize is to comprehend what is real. The evolving human ability to realize and to distinguish what is real through trial and error is continuing to progress yet is far from reaching perfection. With an evolving ability to realize what is real humans reduce dangers in the environment by developing the practical reality of tools and weapons. Dangers of disease have been reduced by realizing and utilizing plants and herbs, and later medicines. Realizing the recurring reality of reducing hunger, humans developed farming methods.

A remaining difficult task for humans is to realize that gods are only subjectively real, that is, they exist in human thinking as artistic imaginations but are not objectively real. A human-like god is a conceived symbol with which to delimit and imagine an arbitrary beginning in a beginningless universe.

A god is an imagined model of human protection, and of human potential to increase knowledge and ability. To realize a god is to comprehend it to be a human conceived egocentric symbol for protection and to encourage human potential.

A human-like god has never saved anyone, only the idea of a human-like god saves by inspiring an individual to look to a higher level of potential and conduct.

Realizing a god, is the inner individual subjective ascension of making ethical choices that elevate an individual from an assortment of poor and lower ethical choices of daily life. Humans subconsciously and consciously shape their lives and are responsible not only for their conscious willing behaviors but also of comprehending subconscious content and body function. Each individual must accept the burden of effort to explore their individual life and observe how self-conscious attention is often clouded, distracted, directed, and dominated by a subconscious triune soul, of hunger for food, sex and reproduction, and aggression.

Much of the human population lives a waking sleep of story, a personal life story based on memory of good and bad experiences, and also a childish imaginary tale of how a human-like god made the environment and human life. In the past and continuing today, theists have reduced the dangers of life by subjectively and falsely imagining and regressing numerically to a human-like first father god who made the environment and the first humans. In the feeble mode of theistic thinking, a human-like first father god of humans must care for them, yet seldom demonstrates it during the course of life. This mode of primitive thinking will no longer suffice in modern times.

The practice of meditation develops a focus of attention that differs from the average attention span. Consistent meditation practice contributes to realizing what is real by increasing a focus of attention. Meditation develops an enhanced elevating ability for perception and better comprehension to distinguish conscious self and the subconscious soul. Meditation removes conscious self limitations imposed by the subconscious triune soul of hunger for food, sex and reproduction, and aggression. Meditation can elevate to a higher level and can see the triune soul to be a continuation of a sole cosmological force.

Realizing what is real and what is not, inevitably leads to removing of limitations and conversely leads to an elevation, a sense of rising up, or of meeting a higher being, that in reality is a level of personal freedom, creativity, and intelligence. Learning about health removes the limitations of illness. Learning to increase financial security removes the limitations of poverty. Free of limiting habit and often stifling social traditions, the resulting elevation enables clear comprehension of the real subjective psychological process of creating imagined gods. Free of distraction, an individual may also elevate to a higher level to realize, to see a real triune soul that forces life to exist.

To realize a god is to reach a higher human level of seeing what the soul is, and how the triune soul is a continuation of a sole cosmological force. Realizing a god, is to see the truth of the triune soul as resilient and resistant to time and destruction, as the power, the force that forces life to evolve, to resist dissolution, and to continue after death through an afterlife dimension.

To realize a god, is to experience what is higher, not as an outside distant object but as an elevation within by reducing human limitations through an increase of learning, and acquiring much knowledge and wisdom. This indeed is a thrilling accomplishment. To realize a god is to subjectively rise within, to reach elevated levels of reasoning, to reach sensitive intuitive and clairvoyant ability to perceive, and to apperceive the worth and pragmatic function of ideas.

A human-like god is a projected imaginary ally for the higher functioning human cerebral cortex. By conceiving of a human-like god, humans attempt to elevate themselves to what is higher within themselves, the cerebral cortex, and away from the lower triune soul that forces the body to live. In reality, humans can only elevate themselves through their own higher knowledge and learning, not by conceiving an ineffective role model of an imaginary human-like god.

A real earth produces and supports the reproduction of life, consumes the living body through voracious time, or destroys it through aggression of environmental change. The triune soul of life as hunger for food, sex and reproduction, and aggression, is a continuation of this reality process. Therefore, an imaginary companion and role model of a human-like god can only be partially effective in inspiring and bringing about an elevation in human thought and ethical behavior. Humans can better elevate themselves through education, investigating, and comprehending that a human-like god is an imaginary companion and an artistic creation, and that the human soul is a reality to be reckoned with.